S I L E N T

The Evolution of the American Cemetery

C I T I E S

Kenneth T. Jackson
Camilo José Vergara

Photographs by Camilo José Vergara

Princeton Architectural Press
New York

Published by Princeton Architectural Press
37 East Seventh Street
New York, New York 10003
212.995.9620

Printed in Thailand
92 91 90 89 5 4 3 2 1

Edited by Amy S. Weisser.
Designed by Kevin C. Lippert and Amy Weisser.

Special thanks to Ken Botnick, Sheila Cohen, Clare Jacobson, Elizabeth Short, and Ann C. Urban.

Library of Congress Cataloging-in-Publication Data

Jackson, Kenneth T.
Silent Cities : the evolution of the American cemetery / Kenneth T. Jackson, Camilo José Vergara; photographs by Camilo José Vergara.
p. cm.
Bibliography: p.
ISBN 0–910413–22–3
1. Cemeteries—United States. 2. Sepulchral monuments—United States. I. Vergara, Camilo J. II. Title.
GT3203.J33 1989 89–33672
3637'5'0973—dc20 CIP

Acknowledgements *viii*
Introduction *2*

The Evolution of the American Cemetery **9**

Church Graveyards 10
Country Graveyards 12
Grove Street Cemetery 14
Père-Lachaise Cemetery, Paris 16
Elite Garden Cemeteries 18
Spring Grove Cemetery 22
Veterans Cemeteries 24
Arlington National Cemetery 26
Memorial Parks 28
Forest Lawn Memorial Park 30
Ordinary Urban Cemeteries 32
Calvary Cemetery 34
Potter's Fields 36

The Cemetery as a Reflection of Society **39**

A Feeling of Daily Life 40
Classicism in Portraiture 42
Righteousness Portrayed 44
Photographic Portraits 46
Ethnic Representations 48
Italian Americans 50
German Americans 52
Irish Americans 54
Jewish Americans 56
Hispanic Americans 58
Family Plots 60
Vanderbilt Family Cemetery 62
Monuments to Marriage 64
Memorials to Children 66
Plots for Organizations 68

Designing for Eternity **71**

Cemetery Entrances 72
Classical Revivals 74
Medieval Revivals 78
Egyptian Revivals 80
Old World Images of Death 82
American Images of Death 84
Images of Grief 86
Images of Voluptuousness 88
Crosses 90
Resurrection Angels 92
Landscapes 94

The Contemporary Cemetery **97**

The Cemetery as a Business 98
Neglected Cemeteries 100
Eroded Monuments 102
Highgate Cemetery, London 104
Alternative Uses of Cemeteries 106
Visiting the Grave 108
The Rise of Cremation 110
Mausolea and Columbaria 112
Bohemian National Cemetery 114

Conclusion *118*
Bibliography *124*

Acknowledgements

Like most books, *Silent Cities* has resulted from the collaboration and assistance of many people, most of whom are nowhere mentioned in the text. In the course of a seven year investigation, hundreds of groundskeepers, monument makers, cemetery administrators, and mourners shared their observations about the changing ways in which Americans remember and memorialize their dead. It was a monument maker, for example, who called our attention to "the lady in black," an attractive middle-aged woman from the Bronx who spends all day, every day, winter and summer, rain or shine, at the grave of her mother in Kensico Cemetery in Valhalla, New York. We hope that, in our search for large patterns, we have not lost sight of the uniqueness in us all. "The lady in black" is not typical of anyone in the contemporary United States, but her solitary vigil is a reminder that some people still regard the cemetery as a place where the living and the dead can communicate.

More than anyone other than the two authors, Lisa Vergara has helped bring this book into being. Her familiarity with the symbols and forms used to commemorate the dead, her keen eye to detect meanings in photographs and to select the clearest and most forceful images, and her help in formulating ideas have all contributed immensely to our study.

Frank Vos read our manuscript at an early stage and made very valuable suggestions regarding its organization, style and form. Barbara B. Jackson, Douglas Curry, and Daniel Bluestone read parts of the manuscript and gave useful comments. Amy Weisser, our editor at Princeton Architectural Press, did much to reinforce the logic of our argument and the consistency of our presentation. Kevin Lippert deserves special thanks for his courage and independence of mind in publishing this book.

A grant from the Design Arts Program of the National Endowment for the Arts was essential in supporting our travel and photography. Similarly, this book would not have been possible without access to the collections of the Avery Library of Columbia University. In particular, bibliographers Herbert Mitchell and William O'Malley deserve thanks for calling our attention to a wide range of useful sources.

Earlier versions of *Silent Cities* were presented to audiences at Union Theological Seminary, Columbia University, the Brooklyn Historical Society, the University of California at Los Angeles, the University of California at Berkeley, and the Museum of the City of New York. The authors gratefully acknowledge the suggestions and criticisms which were willingly shared at these sessions.

Dating monuments is a difficult, often impossible, task. Cemetery administrators have surprisingly little information about grave markers on their grounds, and even when the information is at hand, they are reluctant to share it, claiming respect for the wishes of the family. Dealing with the large number of monuments in this book, we were unable to give precise dates for every marker. From several administrators, however, we learned that the tendency has long been to install monuments within a year of the first burial. We therefore have recorded the date of the earliest burial, except when the exact date is known to us from other sources.

When, in a caption, a date appears prior to the name and location of the cemetery, the date is that of the monument. When the date is listed following the location, it refers to the date the picture was taken.

Introduction

Where we were, you are. What we are, you will become.

Behold my grave as you pass by. As you are living so once was I. Death suddenly took hold of me, And so will be the case with thee.

Young friends regard this solemn Truth. So you may die like me in youth. Death is a debt to nature due, Which I have paid, and so must you.

Behould and See
For as I am
Soe shalt Thou Be
But as Thou Art
Soe Once Was I
Bee Sure of This
That Thou Must Dye.

These recurrent epitaphs, which can be found in seventeenth- and eighteenth-century cemeteries throughout the United States, remind us of the universal certainty of human existence: In the midst of life, we are in death. Members of the American Cryonics Society dispute this assertion. They argue that death is not final. By freezing the body of a person immediately after death, they hope to preserve it until somewhere, somehow and someday, scientists find a cure for whatever killed the poor soul and bring the departed back to life.

Despite the hope of Cryonics members, the Grim Reaper will not be denied. There are exceptions to every rule except this last one—whatever our age, sex or religion, whatever our race, nationality or class, our fate is to return to dust. An English humorist has warned, "Don't take life too seriously; you won't get out of it alive," while the famous words of Ecclesiastes state poetically and clearly our inevitable mortality: "To every thing there is a season, and a time to every purpose under the heaven: A time to be born and a time to die."

This book is about the time to die or, more precisely, the aftermath of dying. Human beings are unique among the earth's creatures in their awareness that there is a natural and inescapable end to life and in their elaboration of formal rituals to accompany the disposal of the corpse. Funerary practices are usually invested with enormous psychological and emotional significance. As French architect and theorist Eugene Viollet-le-Duc noted a century ago: "Of all monuments, tombs are those that present perhaps the broadest subject for the study of the archaeologist, historian, artist, even philosopher. Civilizations, at every step of the ladder, have manifested the nature of their beliefs in another life by the way in which they have treated the dead." These sentiments have been endorsed by anthropologist Clifford Geertz, who has explained that attitudes regarding death have always been closely related to social life. As Geertz noted in *The Interpretation of Cultures*, "[We] have never been able to study humans seriously without considering the essential fact of their mortality. This is because death and its rituals not only reflect social values, but are an important force in shaping them."

Every period in history and every land mass on the globe provide evidence that cemeteries are collective representations of deeply shared attitudes and assumptions. The Celtics, for example, believed that a deceased person without a grave became a vampire, while residents of prehistoric Jericho treasured the actual skulls of their forebears. Similarly, during the Shang Dynasty in China, a high regard for the spirit of the departed led to the custom of providing the corpse with all possible earthly possessions and services, even if preparation required human sacrifice. One of the tombs excavated at Wu-kuan-ts'un was littered with the skeletons of twenty-two men and twenty-four women; fifty more skulls were buried in adjacent pits.

Other traditions and cultures have placed a premium on physical proximity. Ancient Greeks and Romans often buried their dead under the floor of their houses, a practice that continues today on the Ivory Coast, where little distinction is made between the space of the living and that of the dead. Here, each family keeps its lifeless members close by in the hut or the vegetable garden. On the South American continent, scholars have long been impressed by the exceptional structures the Incas erected for the deceased. Alongside their precariously built houses, the Incas' tombs represent the summit of Incan architecture. Even today, their dirt-poor descendants regard a burial plot as one of the most desirable of possessions.

Immigrant groups in the United States revealed an attitude toward the importance of a proper funeral and a respectable burial similar to that of the Incas. Thus, families who counted every coin nevertheless made whatever sacrifices necessary to join a local burial society. Impoverished

Pallbearers carrying the coffin of Kenneth Gordon Jackson II into the Presbyterian Church of Mount Kisco, New York; 1984.

blacks repeated this pattern, and black benevolent organizations grew up to assure members a proper interment. In New Orleans, for example, such groups held special rites over the body, hired bands to lead funeral processions, marched in special regalia, and assumed burial expenses. They even fined members who failed to attend the wakes of their associates.

The obvious fact that there has never been a single attitude toward mortality among all the earth's peoples reflects economic and geographic realities as well as religious and cultural attitudes. According to Francis Parkman, a prominent nineteenth-century historian, Dakotah Indians honored dead warriors by placing them in trees, where vultures could separate flesh from bone. In contemporary India, both religious belief and scarcity of land have created a pattern in which the deceased are consumed on huge funeral pyres, obviating the need to relegate space for a cemetery.

Throughout most of history and for most of the earth's peoples, however, the preferred place for disposing of the body has been the cemetery. This tradition of burial in a sacred place dates back thousands of years. Ancient Egyptians regarded it as dishonorable to deprive the dead of proper burial, while in Rome even the humblest citizen could recite: *Sit tibi terra levis* (May the earth lie lightly on these remains). Lewis Mumford argued that the city of the dead, in fact, antedates the city of the living. As he wrote in *The City in History:*

The dead were the first to have a permanent dwelling,...[a place] to which the living [could return regularly to visit their ancestors].

...Food-gathering and hunting [did] not encourage the permanent occupation of a single site, the dead at least claim that privilege. Long ago the Jews claimed as their patrimony the land where the graves of their forefathers were situated; and that well-attested claim seems a primordial one....[Thus], the city of the dead is the forerunner, almost the core, of every living city.

Cemeteries, then, are visible manifestations of human mortality. Their very existence is an admission of our own frail and transitory being, a reminder that there is an end to life and that we "are strangers and sojourners here." When there is no cemetery, when a loved one must be interred in a distant or remote spot, the loss seems especially poignant. Parkman recalled that the Oregon Trail was lined with the graves of those who had become sick and died along the way: "One morning, a piece of plank, standing upright on the summit of a grassy hill, attracted our notice, and riding up to it, we found the following words traced upon it, apparently with a red hot piece of iron: MARY ELLIS, DIED MAY 7TH, 1845, AGED TWO MONTHS. Such tokens were of common occurrence." Similarly, travelers today over the towering mountain passes along the remote Karakoram Highway, between China and Pakistan, encounter as they approach Islamabad a tablet simple in its grief, yet powerful in its reminder of how the harsh geography has so often triumphed over man. "In loving memory of our only son, Harold S. Elrod," the inscription reads, "Captain, Sikh Pioneers, Kashmir Infantry, accidentally drowned while fording the Indus, December 1, 1929, aged 33. Until the day breaks and the shadows flee away."

We mourn the many; we mourn the one.

Silent Cities focuses on the evolution of cemeteries in what is now the United States. It makes no claim to comprehensiveness. There are more than 150,000 burial places of all types in this country, and a single volume cannot hope to portray even a fraction of them in all their diversity. Instead, this book is based upon an examination of over three hundred cemeteries in twenty-one states—among them the oldest, largest, poorest, and ethnically most diverse—and upon interviews with more than a hundred monument dealers, funeral directors, groundskeepers, cemetery officials, and bereaved visitors. Although incomplete, and in places very painfully so, it represents one of the more comprehensive examinations of American cemeteries yet attempted. This is a reflection of the fact that, until recently, few scholars have been attracted to the subject. Even anthropologists, who have made elaborate studies of the burial practices of remote tribes, have virtually ignored the rituals of the American people. Only in the last two decades, following a renewed interest in death and dying inspired by the "Annales school" of history in France and especially by Philippe Aries and Michel Vovelle, have books and articles that go substantially beyond the anecdotal and the antiquarian appeared on the cemetery. Previous work in this field concentrated on particular famous places, such as Arlington or Forest Lawn, on colonial churchyards, or on the graves of the rich and famous. More recently, however, Richard Etlin, Blanche Linden-Ward, J.B. Jackson, Thomas Bender, James J. Farrell, David Schuyler, Stanley French, David Stannard, Allan I. Ludwig, and John R. Stilgoe, among others, have moved burial grounds out of a narrow framework and into the mainstream of American scholarship.

Silent Cities differs from recent analytical work in two ways. First, it does not focus exclusively or even predominantly on the elite "rural" or "garden" cemeteries, such as Mount Auburn in Cambridge, Spring Grove in Cincinnati, Green-Wood in Brooklyn, Graceland in Chicago, Elmwood in Memphis, and Mount Hope in Rochester, which so transformed the funerary customs of wealthy Americans in the nineteenth century. These pastoral pleasure grounds were the precursors of public parks, and they provided a place where visitors could escape the grime and bustle of urban life for the serenity of a garden displaying the best in art and architecture. Like their illustrious counterparts in Europe, notably Père-Lachaise in Paris, Highgate in London, and Staglieno in Genoa, many have their own book-length, official histories, and they have all attracted the attention of serious researchers in recent years. Instead, we have attempted to bring to the fore the ordinary urban cemetery. Such places have always been less pastoral than their more expensive cousins, but the average turn-of-the-century Chicagoan was interred in the crowded confines of a place like Mount Carmel rather than among the Gettys, the Ryersons, and the Burnhams in expensive Graceland. Every major city had, for example, a large, Catholic, working-class cemetery that met the needs of a first and second generation immigrant community. In New York, the official burial ground of the Archdiocese is called Calvary, and it has already accommodated 2.3 million bodies, or more than the combined total of the six largest "rural" cemeteries in North America.

Second, *Silent Cities* does not examine the tombs of the rich and famous. There is within us all, as John Betjeman noted in *Harrap's Guide to Famous London Graves*, a natural hero-worshipping instinct which likes to see where the remains of those we admired or loved are buried. The authors of this book share this curiosity and have stood over or beside all that is mortal of Babe Ruth, Marilyn Monroe, Walt Whitman, Louis Sullivan, John F. Kennedy, Jim Morrison, and dozens of others of similar fame. But books and articles in large number are already available to satisfy this craving, and *Silent Cities* does not seek to expand upon them.

This book, instead, has five main purposes. The first is to provide a categorization of burial places that have evolved in the United States. Most people have noticed that cemeteries differ in function, appearance and size, but this is the first systematic effort to trace the history and assess the significance of all the different types and, most especially, of the huge ethnic burial grounds of great American cities.

Second, we seek to show that the cemetery is one place where America has tried to present and celebrate its history. Blanche Linden-Ward has argued that the need for commemoration, for a visual record of the nation's history, arose with the greatest intensity in nineteenth-century Boston. It was no coincidence that those who pressed for an appropriate monument to mark the Bunker Hill battlefield were among the same people who later would play a central role in the creation of Mount Auburn, America's first "rural" cemetery. The revolutionary nature of these aspirations becomes apparent when one recalls that the eighteenth-century tomb of George Washington was not even inscribed with his name, and that in 1851, when R.A. Smith visited the grave of Benjamin Franklin at Christ Church Burial Place in Philadelphia, he found it "in a sad and neglected state." Linden-Ward suggested that a full-scale "commemorative consciousness" emerged in the 1830s when civic leaders decided to honor the great men who had lived among them by building monuments to their memory. The monuments in cemeteries fulfill a range of inspirational, patriotic and historical needs. As we consider the evolution of American burial places we frequently must focus attention on commemoration as a common aspiration.

Grave digger shoveling dirt in the traditional manner as he opens a grave for a small child; Lincoln Cemetery, Compton, California, 1987.

The third purpose of *Silent Cities* is to analyze the ways in which burial places and markers reflect social and class structure as well as ordinary attitudes and popular tastes. It is a truism that death imitates life, that funerary monuments are a reflection of earthly states. The corpses of the indigent typically have been treated in a cavalier manner. For example, in the middle of the nineteenth century, the Campo Santo in Naples was devoted almost exclusively to the destitute and the friendless. A low wall enclosed a quadrangular area divided into 365 vaults, or pits—one for every day of the year; each pit was covered with a marble slab with a massive iron ring fastened in the center. When the anniversary of one of these holes arrived, the cover was removed, and in the evening, carts appeared with that day's dead; the dead were tossed without clothes or coffin into the darkness below, almost as a porter would pitch a sack of grain. When the last of the dead had been so dispatched, a load of quick lime was thrown over the bodies. The hole was not opened again for a year, by which time only a heap of bones reposed at the bottom of the pit.

At the opposite end of the social scale, the rich and well-born have always made impressive efforts to insure that appropriate ceremony and style accompanies their spirit throughout eternity. In no case is the example more extreme than the three great pyramids at Giza. Requiring millions of hours of effort, the smooth-sided pyramids mark the high point of Pharaonic power. The three were more elaborate than any structures designed for the living; the largest measured 13 acres at the base and 482 feet in height (equivalent to a 48-story building). While the pyramids have stood in the Valley of the Nile for almost five thousand years, they have been plundered by historians and archaeologists, and the Pharaohs would hardly be happy with the result.

One of the exquisite tombs of modern times is Napoleon's in Paris, and in our century, the most grandiose is Chiang Kai-Shek's in Taipei. The Chinese peasants that Chiang Kai-Skek ruled live in places and in circumstances that reflect the poverty of their human existence; meanwhile, the Generalissimo rests in a blue and white tomb so immense and so opulent that the Taiwanese themselves regard it as an embarrassment. Ironically, Chairman Mao Tse-Tung, the architect and leader of the Communist Revolution in Asia, a man who espoused egalitarianism all his long life, is preserved under glass in marble and granite splendor at the center of Tianamen Square in Beijing. The situation is no different in the Soviet Union, where rank is as important in death as it is in life. Interment in Moscow's Novodevichy Cemetery, once reserved for the brightest luminaries of Czarist Russia, currently requires a favorable decision by the Politburo; the Kremlin Wall proves to be an even more exclusive, and therefore more prestigious, necropolis.

Grave site prepared for the lowering of a casket. The grave and the chairs for the mourners are covered with a green material so as to blend in with the lawn; Rose Hill Cemetery, Chicago, Illinois, 1983.

The United States does not contain any funerary monuments on the scale of that of the ancient Pharaohs nor any burial places as restricted as Novodevichy or the Kremlin Wall, but no other nation even approaches ours in the overall number and size of its cemeteries or in the total sum of money expended on the disposal of its dead. Woodlawn Cemetery in the Bronx, for example, is one of America's largest, most beautiful, and most famous cemeteries, and its 400 acres of park-like grounds contain perhaps the greatest variety of graves of historically important individuals anywhere in the nation. J.C. Penny, F.W. Woolworth, R.H. Macy, Joseph Pulitzer, Herman Melville, Fiorello LaGuardia, Chief Justice Charles Evans Hughes, Duke Ellington, W.C. Handy, George M. Cohen, and Admiral David Farragut are among the 300,000 people buried there. But Woodlawn contains more than grandiose mausoleums by great American architects. Indeed, most of the markers are simple and inexpensive, reflecting the earthly circumstances of the persons who repose beneath them. In particularly stark terms, therefore, Woodlawn duplicates the class structure of the United States. As John Maass has pointed out, Woodlawn, like other cemeteries, has mansions (mausoleums) on large lots with grand approaches and slums (unmarked graves) on back streets. There are single-family homes (ordinary graves) on winding suburban drives (walks) as well as apartment buildings (community mausolea and columbaria) on busy thoroughfares. There are even public buildings (gateways, chapels, offices) on squares and fashionable boulevards.

Maass did not mention that American cemeteries also have religious and racial ghettoes. Observant Jews, Catholics and Mormons rest in the sacred ground of their separate faiths, while black and white Americans have been separated in death even more than in life. Indeed, few epitaphs anywhere are as memorable as that of Thaddeus Stevens (1792-1868), a white congressman from Pennsylvania whose legislative career was especially associated with the struggle for racial equality. His tomb in the small "Negro" graveyard of Lancaster contains the following inscription:

I repose in this quiet and secluded spot,
Not from any natural preference for solitude
But, finding other Cemeteries limited as to Race
by Charter Rules,
I have chosen that I might illustrate
in my death
The Principles which I advocated
Through a long life:
EQUALITY OF MAN BEFORE HIS CREATOR.

For the most part, Americans did not follow Thaddeus Stevens's example, however, and by the end of the nineteenth century, most Southern states had passed legislation to enforce the color line at the grave. Northern cities were not so blatantly prejudiced, but burial grounds above the Mason-Dixon Line were, in fact, almost as segregated as those of the Old South.

In addition to considering the ways in which the cemetery reflects the class, religious and racial distinctions of the larger society, this book analyzes how the changing character of the American family has shaped cemeteries. We look too at organizational loyalties and ethnic patterns in death: commemoration has rarely been considered by historians and anthropologists when studying immigration and assimilation. Focusing on Italians, Jews, the Irish, Germans, and Hispanics, we show how cultural attitudes brought from other nations find expression in the cemetery. Just ten miles from San Francisco, for example, along the old Mission Road in San Mateo County, there were a dozen cemeteries by 1915. Four were Jewish, two were Chinese, and one each was Italian, Hungarian and Japanese.

A fourth purpose of *Silent Cities* is to analyze the results of "designing for eternity." Especially in the nineteenth and early twentieth centuries, the relationship between Christianity and memorialization was everywhere apparent in the typical graveyard; it was expressed in inaugural addresses, on entrance gates and on monuments themselves. Whether one is examining non-denominational "elite rural" cemeteries or "ordinary urban" cemeteries, one finds the belief in the Resurrection in crosses, in images of angels and in quotations from the Bible. As a Pittsburgh clergyman remarked at the interment of war dead in Allegheny Cemetery in 1848: "These bones live—to us, and to our successors is confided the sacred trust of preserving them inviolate, until the last trump[et] shall call the dead to judgement."

Another purpose of *Silent Cities* is to consider the demise of the cemetery as the place where most people expect to be commemorated one day. In the nineteenth century, the most fashionable architects—Richard Morris Hunt, Louis Sullivan, Charles F. McKim, Stanford White, and others—and the most talented sculptors—Augustus St. Gaudens, Lorado Taft, and Daniel Chester French—designed funerary monuments, and prominent national leaders spoke eloquently of the cemetery as a place of inspiration and reflection. Judge Story's comments at Mount Auburn are apposite:

Dust as we are, the frail tenements which enclose our spirits but for a season, are dear, are inexpressibly dear to us. We derive solace, nay pleasure, from the reflection that when the hour of separation comes, these earthly remains will still retain the tender regard of those whom we leave behind;—that the spot, where they shall lie, will be remembered with a fond and soothing reverence; that our children will visit it in the midst of their sorrows; and our kindred in remote generations feel that a local inspiration hovers round it.

Judge Story would be surprised at the inattention of Americans to cemeteries in the late twentieth century. Cemeteries only a few decades old are sometimes overgrown or abandoned while even the best maintained are rarely visited. Even though Oriental, southern European, and Hispanic groups continue to regard the cemetery as central to their lives, in the eyes of the general public, the mausoleum, the monument and the marker have lost their commemorative function. Our book finally concludes with the loss of commemorative customs and the emergence of cremation as an alternative to the traditional cemetery.

Dark uniformly rectangular openings: the grid of a mausoleum under construction; Southern California, 1985.

THE EVOLUTION OF THE AMERICAN CEMETERY

Almost everyone has at least one cemetery frozen in his or her memory. It may be particularly historic, or beautiful, or serene, or ostentatious. It may be famous because of the great and the powerful who are interred there or memorable because of its unusual appearance. Most likely we revere a particular cemetery because it is the final resting place of someone who once shared our life.

Whatever or wherever the cemetery, it probably falls into one or another distinctive category—the country cemetery, the church graveyard, the elite rural cemetery, the ordinary urban cemetery, the veterans cemetery, the memorial park, and the potter's field.

Church Graveyards

Crowded, overgrown colonial graveyard at St. John Episcopal Church, Elizabeth, New Jersey.

...the curate's cow grazes in the village churchyard and feeds his children from his parishioner's remains.

—"Burial," *The North American Review*, 1861

In the olden days the church was used for a graveyard and the planks were removed while the grave was dug. The body was wrapped in a rug and lowered into the grave, which was filled and the boards replaced. This custom prevailed until the entire space was filled with the dead. The floor logs now are twisted and the floor uneven, but it is as solid apparently as ever.

—Resident of Las Trampas, *New Mexico Magazine*, 1933

The large cemetery was unknown in North America prior to the end of the eighteenth century. The deceased usually were interred inside a parish church or in its adjacent burial ground. Of course, the isolated farmer might have been buried in an open field, the agnostic urban resident in an undeveloped city lot or the vagrant in a potter's field, but the majority preferred a place close to a house of God. The church interior itself was especially well regarded, and the rich, the powerful and the influential, as well as the clergy, sought crypts beneath the slabs of the floor, as near to the altar as possible, as had been the case in Europe for centuries.

Burying the departed within the church was inconvenient, however, and the space available was not adequate for the demand. Thus the tradition of using the surrounding grounds developed. The resulting church graveyards were at the center of life, part of the pattern of everyday existence. Simple markers, viewed by passersby on their way to work or to service, functioned as constant reminders of the transitory nature of human life. Indeed, the most common epitaph stated: "Where you are now, so once was I. Where I am now, so you will be."

Although twentieth-century Americans typically regard such church graveyards as picturesque, the colonists tended to view them as foul smelling, unattractive eyesores. Even in 1800, during the young Republic, Yale President Timothy Dwight described one such burial place in Gilford, Connecticut as an "unkempt section of the town common where the graves and fallen markers were daily trampled upon by people and cattle." This critical view of the church graveyard intensified by the middle of the nineteenth century when public health reformers came to regard the space as a source of disease. As a result, burials within city limits were often prohibited after the Civil War.

Although church graveyards remain common in rural and small town America, very few survive in the modern metropolis. Trinity Church Cemetery in lower Manhattan is a particularly well-known exception, a pleasant oasis of green where office workers eat their lunches and listen to music in the shade.

Other church graveyards have managed to survive after undergoing great change. The New Lots Cemetery in Brooklyn, for example, founded in 1824, was originally located in the middle of farmland, across the road from the Dutch Reformed Church with which it was associated. As Brooklyn became populous in the late nineteenth century, the cemetery was forced to move to a site adjacent to the church in order to make room for a school. Twenty-five years ago a new congregation acquired the church, and the house of worship is now located on the edge of a large ghetto. Few Dutch and German descendants of the former settlers continue to be buried in the New Lots Cemetery. Still, according to the caretaker, some view the cemetery as a family heirloom. It is visited by the trustees at least twice a year "to see if it is still there."

Picturesque view of the Swede's Church Cemetery, in Southwark, Pennsylvania. In this mid-nineteenth-century print, the church's sturdiness contrasts with the burial ground's tilted headstones. *Top left*

Small country church and cemetery located at crossroads; Door County, Wisconsin, 1982. *Center*

Bethel Methodist Church and graveyard, erected in 1840; Tottenville, Staten Island, New York. *Bottom left*

New Lots Cemetery in eastern Brooklyn, New York, founded in the first half of the nineteenth century by the Dutch Reformed Church. The names on the tombstones are the same as those given to the streets and subway stops of the surrounding area: Van Siclen, Wyckoff, Snediker, Schenk, Bergen, Cozine. *Right*

Country Graveyards

Clockwise from upper left:
Scattered markers distinguish this country cemetery from the green pastures beyond; Door County, Wisconsin, 1982.

Small, uniform markers on the graves of Amish families. Here, members of the distinctive religious community are buried together; Weldy Cemetery, Napanee, Indiana, 1986.

Cemetery north of Fort Wayne, Indiana, 1986; colorful flags and flowers are tokens of recent visits.

Vertical mail order markers, dating from the time of the first World War, contrast with the flat open fields of North Central Indiana; 1986.

...You can't drive ten miles or fifteen miles without seeing a cemetery. We have at least eight thousand cemeteries in Texas, ...[but] only about two hundred and fifty of them have a telephone....[A]nybody who was anybody fifty or a hundred years ago and had an entourage of twelve to twenty-five people and owned one thousand acres of ground...established a cemetery. That is the reason we have so many cemeteries.
—John T. Bayley, Cemetery administrator, Fort Worth, 1988

Unlike the pattern in Europe and Asia, where cemeteries are few in number, extremely crowded, and hidden behind solid walls, the country cemetery is a familiar sight along the highways of the United States. The outskirts of every city and small town seem to include space for at least one burial ground. Such cemeteries are smaller, more open and more egalitarian than their counterparts in the city. Sometimes on top of a hill, sometimes in a clearing surrounded by woods, they tend to cover less than a dozen acres. Rarely do they include the mausoleums, large obelisks, elaborate statuary, high fences, and ethnic markers so common in urban cemeteries. Their typically unpretentious homemade or mail order markers commemorate a cross section of the citizenry, the first settlers, the foreign-born, and some of the "local boys" killed in battle. They are usually well-kept; the overseer cuts the grass, fences keep cattle out and visitors plant flowers. Tourists, finding the plots historical and picturesque, stop to read the dates when the area was settled and the names, origins and religions of the local residents.

Hand-made signs marking the grave of children who died more than half a century ago; Fish Creek, Door County, Wisconsin, 1982.

Old grave markers are often decorated with implements such as axes, saws, sickles, plows, and hammers, indicators of the deceased's occupation. Recently these motifs have been updated to images of vehicles or farm equipment, as in the case of George Bish of Ligonier, Indiana, who had his truck engraved on his marker. Country scenes of barns, silos, farm houses with smoke curling from the chimney, and the rising sun are other popular motifs in cemeteries serving rural populations.

America's most famous country cemetery is the fictional graveyard of Grover's Corner, New Hampshire, the setting for Act III of Thorton Wilder's *Our Town* (1938). The time is 1913, and the location is "a windy hilltop." Grover's Corner and its lofty cemetery blend together in harmony, combining the living ("the summer people... laughing at the funny words on the tombstones," "the genealogists...up from Boston") and the dead (the Civil War veterans); the present ("There's Joe Stoddard, our undertaker, supervising a new-made grave. And here comes a Grover's Corners boy, who left town to go out West") and the past ("the old stones,—1670, 1680. Strong minded people that came a long way to be independent").

Wilder mused about the function of the graveyard as a temporary place for the deceased: "They're waitin' for something that they feel is comin'. Something important, and great. Aren't they waitin' for the eternal part in them to come out clear?"

Grove Street Cemetery

Clockwise from upper left:
Entrance to the Grove Street Cemetery—a landmark of the Egyptian Revival—designed by Henry Austin in 1845.

Two eighteenth-century headstones—the older one carved with a winged skull, the more recent with a cherub face—brought from the Old Burying Ground and propped against the new cemetery wall.

The Grove Street grid: view of family monuments in fenced plots; early nineteenth century.

In describing New Haven it would be unpardonable not to mention the New Burying Ground.

—Edward Augustus Kendall,
Travels through Part of the United States, 1809

The first cemetery of the modern genus in the United States was established in New Haven, Connecticut in 1796. Grove Street Cemetery, unlike other burial places that had grown without much forethought, was completely planned from the beginning; its gridiron-style layout was derived from the most advanced city plans of the day. The planners divided the ground not into squares but parallelograms and designed the paths so that two carriages could pass one another. Each plot was of exactly the same dimensions, and every grave faced the same direction. Smooth paths and carefully painted rails completed the plan.

Grove Street Cemetery resulted from the need to replace "the unsightly clutter" and unsanitary conditions of the town churchyard. The most important of the project's thirty-two planners, all prominent citizens of New Haven, was Senator James Hillhouse. Hillhouse first considered the possibility of a family graveyard on his own property but decided against the idea because perpetual care was not assured. After the yellow fever epidemic of 1794 and 1795 made conditions in New Haven's original burial ground intolerable, a second alternative became a reality.

A marker with an unusually lengthy inscription, a public *curriculum vitae*; 1959. *Left*

Jane L. Throwbridge monument, 1840s; an angel transports the deceased to join her three children in heaven: "Parting and sorrow they shall know no more." *Right*

Originally called the New Burial Ground, Grove Street Cemetery's six-acre site was enormous by the standards of its day. Later in the nineteenth century, it was expanded to its present twelve acres.

Unlike the church graveyards, Grove Street Cemetery was private, non-denominational and physically removed from the center of town. Its impressive Egyptian-style gate emphasized this new separation and provided the possibility for private ostentation. Grove Street also introduced the concept, then unusual, of purchasing land for burial; interment in church graveyards had been a privilege of membership in a congregation. Of great importance was the cemetery's encouragement of family sections; previously, people were buried in small, individual plots according to their date of death. With this new emphasis, monuments in the New Haven institution were devoted to the assertion of private wealth: large, expensive markers—obelisks, sarcophagi, statues, shafts, and draped urns—were made of fine materials. The family name, prominently displayed, proclaimed a sense of importance and dignity. In old church graveyards, by contrast, individual names are difficult to decipher, and the slate markers are for the most part indistinguishable from one another.

For all the precedents that it set, Grove Street still managed to accommodate the Old Burying Ground that it replaced; many headstones from the earlier graveyard on the upper Green were transferred to Grove Street and set up against the new walls. Described by an early nineteenth-century observer as "lugubrious images of death and desolation," the old markers today humbly stand in sharp contrast to the profusion of larger, more hopeful Victorian monuments signifying salvation and remembrance.

Père-Lachaise Cemetery, Paris

One of the elegantly curving, cobblestone avenues lined with trees and classical mausoleums; late nineteenth century. *Left*

The pointed roofs of hundreds of narrow mausoleums meet the eye. *Top right*

Corner monuments, including a life-sized statue of Anatole de la Forge leading the Parisian people; 1895. *Bottom right*

[Père-Lachaise] reflects infinite credit on the city as well as upon the character of the French people. In all respects it very far surpasses anything of the kind I have ever seen, and the design strongly recommends itself to the imitation of all great cities.

—Nathaniel Carter, *Letters from Europe… in the years 1825, 1826,* 1827

The most influential cemetery of the nineteenth century, Père-Lachaise in Paris, represents "a turning point in one thousand years of Western history." From the Middle Ages to the 1780s, as Richard Etlin has noted, burial grounds in the form of carefully landscaped gardens were "inconceivable." In the nineteenth century, the novel conception of the cemetery and the cultural influence of the French capital helped Père-Lachaise to become a model for the United States and the world.

Begun as a garden cemetery in the eastern part of Paris in 1804, Père-Lachaise was planned on variegated terrain, with hills, flat stretches, large rocks, and dense woods. Initially 48 acres, or eight times as large as the Grove Street Cemetery, it later expanded to 107 acres. Taking full advantage of the topography, architect Alexandre-Theodore Brongniart designed his cemetery so that visitors would anticipate and discover new views around each bend and ridge and would enjoy superb panoramas of the city from the high points on the grounds. By 1850, Père-Lachaise was famous not only for the beauty of its landscape but also for the celebrities interred there and the variety and quality of its monuments.

Ironically, the very popularity of Père-Lachaise undermined its status as a garden cemetery. While the elaborate vegetation and expensive markers grew in harmony for a few decades, by 1825, more than 25,000 monuments were in place. American visitors found Père-Lachaise lacking in comparison to the American rural cemetery. In the 1860s, in the face of the rapidly increasing number of memorials, D.W. Cheever complained that at Père-Lachaise, "the hand of man was too evident." Similarly, the anonymous writer of "Burial" (*The North American Review*, 1861) offered an extended critique of what he perceived as the unnatural character of Père-Lachaise: "Though presided over by a delicate taste, the French graveyard shows too plainly the pruning hand of man. Artificial landscape, prim *parterres* and mathematically clipped bowers give it too much that stiff and constrained aspect which is the failure of Versailles. Ostentatious monuments and sculptured tombs, though exquisitely executed are laid out on streets, instead of scattered about the grounds." The growth continued until the burial ground completely lost the character of a garden cemetery. By 1989, more than one million corpses occupied the grounds.

Families have stopped visiting and bringing flowers to the older sections of Père-Lachaise. However, the cemetery remains one of the major attractions of the city. Signs of life—if not of horticulture—still abound. Hundreds of elegant sculptures continue to look very much alive, even when portraying men and women on the verge of death, in mourning or in deep contemplation.

Although Père-Lachaise is well maintained, many of the century-old monuments are set awry, lettering has disappeared, and the metal doors and crosses have rusted. Nature has molded the geometries of the monuments so that they take on an almost organic shape. The former dirt roads are paved with cobblestones and lined with tall arching trees, their huge trunks and branches echoing the shape of the mausoleums. Memorials, paths and vegetation seem to grow out of cement and merge together. Even in winter, the cemetery has a green patina from lichens growing on the monuments, from the evergreen cypresses and from the oxidation of bronze. The cemetery somehow has remained strong in character, a satisfying whole.

Clockwise from upper left:
Monument to Agathe Moris and her nephew; 1880s.

Ossuary and monument to the dead by Paul-Albert Bartholome; 1899. Men and women, young and old, alone or together, reluctantly move towards the door of death. In 1901, *Park and Cemetery*, called this "the greatest monument erected to the dead in the world."

Always together: tomb of husband and wife; 1859.

One of the curiosities of the cemetery, a realistic bronze statue of Victor Noir, assassinated by Pierre Bonaparte, depicts the journalist after his death, his head fractured by a bullet; 1890.

An elegant angel highlights a richly decorated mausoleum door.

Elite Garden Cemeteries

The profusion of soaring monuments, resulting from competition among wealthy Philadelphians at the turn of the century, has transformed the original rural character of Laurel Hill Cemetery; late nineteenth century, Philadelphia, Pennsylvania. *Left*

Visitors stroll in the bucolic landscape—with well-spaced, unobtrusive graves—of John Smillie's mid-nineteenth-century print of Brooklyn's Green-Wood Cemetery; New York. *Top right*

Luxuriant plantings surrounding a peaceful pond; Mount Auburn Cemetery, Cambridge, Massachusetts, 1983. *Center*

1903, Forest Hills Cemetery, Duluth, Minnesota. *Bottom right*

Why should we expose our burying grounds to the broad glare of day, to the unfeeling gaze of the idler, to the noisy press of business, to the discordant shouts of merriment or to the baleful visitations of the dissolute?

—Judge Joseph Story, dedication,
Mount Auburn Cemetery, Cambridge, 1832

The American "garden" or "rural" cemetery movement began in 1831 with the consecration of Mount Auburn Cemetery in Cambridge, Massachusetts. Initially proposed by Dr. Jacob Bigelow in 1825 and laid out by Henry A.S. Dearborn, it featured an Egyptian gate and fence, a Norman tower and a granite chapel. As a planned oasis on the outskirts of the city, Mount Auburn defined a new kind of "romantic" cemetery landscape, replete with winding paths and deep forest shade in a natural setting. It represented a reaction against the church graveyard, which at least in large cities had become overcrowded and unattractive, and responded to public health concerns about cemeteries within the confines of a metropolis.

Mount Auburn was an immediate success and gave rise to the establishment of garden cemeteries in many cities in the middle decades of the nineteenth century. Beautiful, secluded and spacious, these cemeteries occupy some of the most spectacular urban settings in America—overlooking Puget Sound in Seattle, San Francisco Bay in Oakland, the Pacific Ocean in Santa Barbara, New York Harbor in Brooklyn, the Mississippi in St. Louis, the Schuylkill in Philadelphia, and the Charles River in

Cambridge. Lavish plantings, ponds, hills, and groves line their many serpentine roads.

Rural cemeteries were elitist in nature; their artistic effect depended on spacious plots and large monuments that people of modest means could not afford. Those of the working class were buried away from the lakes and hills of the privileged in the cemetery's least desirable locations, the areas for individual graves near fences, storage sheds and stables. Yet these rural cemeteries had a populist side as well. From the start, they were heavily visited, not just by the families of the deceased, but by a growing urban population in need of recreation; they were, in essence, America's first large-scale public open spaces. By the 1840s, for example, Victorian Brooklynites could travel by direct horse car to famed Green-Wood Cemetery. Once there, visitors strolled the grounds, guidebook in hand, viewing sculptural tombs, enjoying fresh air, and picnicking along undulating paths. In 1866, the *New York Times* described Green-Wood as one of Brooklyn's greatest attractions, on a par with Manhattan's Central Park or Fifth Avenue. The rural cemetery movement met with such public approval that it inspired the American park movement and encouraged the professionalization of landscape architecture.

Life-sized statue of a graceful, reflective maiden bringing flowers to a tomb; Riverview Cemetery, Trenton, New Jersey. *Left*

At Mount Pleasant Cemetery, a flowery spring scene not to be found elsewhere in Newark, New Jersey, 1982. *Right*

One of the most lavish of all mausoleum groupings in the United States; late nineteenth–early twentieth century, Laurel Hill Cemetery, Philadelphia, Pennsylvania.

Most important, rural cemeteries reflected a strong feeling for nature. D.B. Douglass, first president of Green-Wood Cemetery, stated that the cemetery's name implied associations of "verdure, shade, ruralness, natural beauty." In 1839, he explained why he could not rename the cemetery "Necropolis," as some had advised. The latter term, he explained, "classic as it is...*savours* of *art* and *classic refinement*, rather than of *feeling*, and herein is our objection.—A *Necropolis* should be an architectural establishment, not a shady forest....[A] Necropolis is a mere depository for *dead bodies*—ours is a *Cemetery*...a *place of repose*."

Not surprisingly, rural cemeteries included wide varieties of trees and shrubs; Mount Auburn initially was planned as an arboretum. Similarly, a 1985 New York survey disclosed that Woodlawn Cemetery in the Bronx had a larger number of "remarkable trees" than Central Park, which is twice Woodlawn's size. The cult of trees and plants is evident even from the names given to the streets of such cemeteries—Lilac Lane, Rhododendron Alley, Sycamore Avenue, and the like.

The administration of the rural cemeteries did not leave the selection and placement of trees and plants to the vagaries of individual fancy. The *Rules and Regulations of Green-Wood Cemetery* (1839) advised families that "good judgment and taste should prevail." As for flowers: "Nothing coarse and incongruous with the object and the place

should be chosen. Those which are delicate in size, form and color should be preferred. Such as are simple and unobtrusive, and particularly those which are symbolical of friendship, affection, and remembrance, seem most fitting to beautify the Place of Graves." The important considerations were the establishment of a sense of decorum and the guarantee of a rich and varied landscape.

The Englishwoman Harriet Martineau, writing in the first half of the nineteenth century, saw "every step teeming with the promise of life" in Mount Auburn. The crowding of monuments at Père-Lachaise, on the other hand, seemed to Martineau to create an overwhelming feeling of hopeless mourning and little sense of the continuity of life. She felt that the weight of the monuments kept nature from growing and the dead from rising. The sentiments of a Boston editorialist writing about Mount Auburn in 1831 were similar to Martineau's; its designers, he thought, had created "a village of the quick and the silent, where Nature throws an air of cheerfulness over the labors of Death."

Mausoleum in a severe classical style; Woodlawn Cemetery, the Bronx, New York. *Top left*

Declared a Chicago landmark in 1971, the Getty mausoleum designed by Louis Sullivan is a masterpiece of modern architecture. According to the Commission of Chicago Historical and Architectural Landmarks: "Here the architect departed from historical precedent to create a building of strong geometric massing, detailed with original ornament;" 1890, Graceland Cemetery, Chicago, Illinois. *Bottom left*

Victorian mausoleums; Laurel Hill Cemetery, Philadelphia, Pennsylvania. *Right*

Spring Grove Cemetery

This pond, teeming with fishes and frogs, explores the idea of the cemetery as a preserve of nature within the reach of city dwellers. *Left*

Jacob Burnet's mausoleum, built in 1865 of Italian marble, recalls the grand portals of Roman palaces and churches. *Right*

We are advancing rapidly...[T]he teachings and doctrines of many of our public-spirited men and civic organizations which lead us on to live our lives under more beautiful conditions and attractive surroundings have fallen upon a receptive public mind...[One] result...along these lines is the modern park-like cemetery. Almost with shame we look back to the days of our forefathers, when the cemetery was considered the most forlorn, neglected and shunned spot on earth in our communities, a place fit for nothing else than the "goblins" to roam about, the lonely owl to screech in, or the serpent to hiss among fallen tombstones, dry leaves and brush.

—Carl A. Kern, Assistant Superintendent,
Spring Grove Cemetery, Cincinnati, 1915

One of the largest and most beautiful cemeteries in the United States is Spring Grove in Cincinnati, Ohio. Established in 1844 and designed by Howard Daniels on the model of Mount Auburn, Green-Wood and Laurel Hill, Spring Grove later introduced a new concept, called the "lawn plan," in which landscape took precedence over monuments and included varied and surprising vistas. Comprising 733 acres, Spring Grove has fewer monuments in twice the space of Cambridge's Mount Auburn.

In 1855, Adolph Strauch, a Prussian-born gardener with extensive experience in Europe, became the superintendent of Spring Grove; he soon helped the cemetery earn a national reputation as an arboretum. Strauch rerouted roads to follow the natural contours of the land, and he encouraged lot owners to authorize removal of hedgerows and fences from around grave sites. Strauch's lawn plan was intended to maintain a feeling of openness and to dot the grounds with lakes, islands and footbridges. He was one of the first to encourage a combination of large lots and small monuments and to suggest

low-maintenance markers that would not impede extensive landscaping and sweeping vistas.

The true character of Spring Grove reveals itself only after the visitor passes from the entry area, through a tunnel under a railroad line, into the mysterious landscape. The monuments, small in size and number, are overwhelmed by trees. A large, undeveloped "Woodland Area" at the center of the cemetery complements the neatly trimmed lawns. Several ponds reflect the surrounding trees, and their calm, level surfaces pleasantly interrupt the hilly terrain.

In a tribute to Strauch in *Park and Cemetery* magazine in 1896, John B. Peaslee noted the difficulty of transforming a dreary graveyard into a park. "When [Strauch] began to remove the fences around the graves and otherwise to change, I should say revolutionize, the graveyard in accordance to the 'park plan'...letters threatening his life were sent to him, and article after article appeared in the Cincinnati papers condemnatory of his course." Strauch's efforts were eventually vindicated. A commission appointed by the French government to visit and examine the parks and cemeteries of the world declared Spring Grove "the most beautiful of all cemeteries."

Clockwise from upper left:
Civil War Memorial

Sculpted figures sit, plead and contemplate by a serene lake.

Lienenbrink family monument, circa 1900.

Landscape with undulating lawns.

Veterans Cemeteries

Spanish-American War section, with markers arranged around a statue of *The Hiker*, a symbol of the American soldier during that war; 1899, Fairmount Cemetery, Denver, Colorado. *Left*

Civil War section, Easton Cemetery, Easton, Pennsylvania. *Right*

On fame's eternal camping grounds
His silent tent is spread,
And glory guards with solemn rounds
The bivouac of the dead.

—Epitaph for Union officer Alexander Hays, Allegheny Cemetery, Pittsburgh, 1864

The first large military cemetery in the United States was established in south central Pennsylvania in 1863, shortly after the Battle of Gettysburg insured the doom of the Confederacy. It was here that President Lincoln gave his famous Gettysburg Address, with its memorable lines: "...we cannot dedicate—we cannot consecrate—we cannot hallow—this ground. The brave men, living and dead, who struggled here, have consecrated it, far above our poor power to add or detract."

By 1989 there were one hundred and ten such cemeteries in the United States, containing more than a million nearly identical white markers. (In newer military burial grounds, flat markers are set flush against rolling lawns.) Uniform greenness and openness, an orderly pattern of

markers and a general absence of visitors characterize the cemeteries. Generally, the placid setting contrasts markedly with the noisy surroundings: fast moving highways dotted with motels, restaurants and gas stations and cluttered with billboards.

National military cemeteries were established for the burial or cremation of honorably discharged veterans and their immediate families. Eleven percent of those who are eligible choose military cemeteries as their final resting place. Veterans preferring a civilian cemetery can obtain a regulation gravestone or plaque and an allowance to help pay for the burial plot.

At a military funeral an American flag is draped over the coffin before its transport to a preassigned section of the cemetery. "Military honors" are given to a service person who dies in active duty: these honors include the mournful sound of taps, a seven-person honor guard and a final rifle volley in salute. The ceremony concludes when the flag is removed from the coffin and presented on behalf of a grateful nation to the closest surviving relative.

Clockwise from left:
Civil War military section of Allegheny Cemetery, Pittsburgh, Pennsylvania; a tall monument crowned by a statue of a sorrowful woman in classical garb is encircled by cannons and white markers.

World War II memorial placed along the main cemetery road by the American Legion; Woodlawn Memorial Cemetery, Miami, Florida.

Golden Gate National Cemetery, one of the largest military cemeteries in the United States; San Bruno, California, 1984.

Arlington National Cemetery

Memorial gate by McKim, Mead and White, flanked by imperious eagles; 1932, Arlington National Cemetery, Washington, D.C. *Left*

Rows of the approximately 170,000 white headstones in the cemetery. *Right*

Nothing could be more impressive than the rank after rank of white stones, inconspicuous in themselves, covering the gentle wooded slopes and producing the desired effect of a vast army in its last resting place.

—Augustus St. Gaudens,
on Arlington National Cemetery, 1901

Arlington National Cemetery, attracting more than four million visitors a year, is easily the most famous burial place in the United States. Originally the farm and mansion of George Washington Parke Custis (stepson of George Washington), the property passed in 1831 to the family of Robert E. Lee, who had married Custis's daughter. During the Civil War the estate was taken by the United States government, and the mansion was used as a hospital. In 1864, Secretary of War Edwin McMasters Stanton declared Arlington a cemetery.

Arlington's 612 acres include hills, valleys and over twenty thousand trees. Unlike the newer national cemeteries, which are not segregated by rank and which feature homogenous flat markers, at Arlington an officer section with elaborate nineteenth-century monuments stands apart from the uniform graves of lower-ranked service people. From the top of one hill an equestrian statue of General Kearny surveys the "troops" waiting in perfect formation below. Until 1948, racial segregation also ruled the burial ground. Although Arlington resulted from a

Emerson Hamilton's monument with a heroic classical figure of a victorious warrior. *Left*

E.C. Potter's bronze equestrian statue of Brigidier General Philip Kearny; 1914. *Right*

war which ended slavery, it conformed to the separation of grave sites for blacks and whites typical of military cemeteries until President Truman desegregated the armed forces by executivé order.

A view from the Custis Lee mansion, elevated on a hill in the cemetery, reveals the succession of great national monuments on the Washington Mall. From the center of the city, the Capitol building, the memorials to Washington, Lincoln, Jefferson, and those who fell in the War in Vietnam all point visitors to Arlington Memorial Bridge and across the Potomac River. Here, the John F. Kennedy grave, with its perpetual flame, the Tomb of the Unknown Soldier, the burial spaces of three hundred recipients of the Medal of Honor, and tens of thousands of small white markers in the undulating landscape provide a meaningful terminus to the landscape of patriotism lying before it.

Long Island National Cemetery in New York may be the largest military burial ground in the United States, but Arlington National Cemetery remains without equal. England offers the model of Westminster Abbey, and France has the Pantheon. Green-Wood in Brooklyn, Mount Auburn in Cambridge, Lake View in Cleveland, and more recently Forest Lawn in Southern California have tried to create an American Pantheon, a place of inspiration for ordinary people, where the memory of great men and women is preserved. Despite the dignity and significance of these places, the center of commemoration in the United States is clearly the space, the monuments and the memorials that run continuously from the Washington Mall to Arlington Cemetery.

Memorial Parks

Clockwise from upper left:
Memorial park on a hill overlooking the Meadowlands; northern New Jersey.

A coffin awaiting burial interrupts Lincoln Cemetery's flat brown lawn; Compton, California.

Small planters with flowers add color to this memorial park section of Greenwood Cemetery; Superior, Wisconsin.

Flat markers from the 1960s and 1970s surrounded by the hills of San Bruno; Holy Cross Cemetery, Colma, California, 1985.

We have our cemeteries, as often as not flat, grassy lawns with almost no visible evidence of the names and family relationships or special qualities of those who are interred beneath.

—David E. Stannard, historian

Visitors come from everywhere; I wish that they may go home to remodel their local cemeteries after the pattern of Forest Lawn—a noble resting place for the departed and a perpetual delight for those who live. Not until that happens will we be able to call ourselves a truly Christian nation.

—Bruce Barton, "Pictorial Forest Lawn," 1944

Early in 1917, Dr. Hubert Eaton began what would later become the vast Forest Lawn complex in Southern California. Working in suburban Glendale, he proposed "...a great park, devoid of misshapen monuments and other customary signs of earthly death, but filled with towering trees, sweeping lawns, splashing fountains, singing birds, beautiful statuary, cheerful flowers, noble memorial architecture with interiors full of light and color, and redolent of the world's best history and romance." The result was a burial place that came to serve as a model for memorial parks across the United States. The requirement that memorial tablets be flush with the ground, thus making lawn care more economical and giving greater prominence to the park-like landscape, became its essential feature.

Although memorial parks proliferated in the two decades after 1917, first- and second-generation immigrant groups continued to prefer above-ground memorials for at least another half century. Only after World War II, when most Americans lost interest in both cemeteries and

monuments, did memorial parks become the dominant type of funerary landscape. Changing patterns of living made the practicality of memorial parks appealing. As J.B. Jackson explains, they are places "where one aspect of death—the disposal of the corpse—is promptly and efficiently taken care of." He adds "The memorial park is particularly valuable to transients who will soon move on and perhaps never see the grave again."

While individual monuments are outlawed at memorial parks, large mass-produced statues are used as decoration at entrances, crossroads and in newer sections of the parks. Most are non-denominational and bear such names as "The Sundial," "Protection Group," "Temple of Love," "Wind Chimes Tower," and "Armed Forces Group." More overtly Christian sculptures often deal with the power of Christ to protect mankind, such as "The Christus," "Christ Stilling the Waters" and "The Good Shepherd"; typically only two are concerned with death—a Pietà group (the dead Christ on Mary's lap) and Christ at Mount Olive.

Few memorial parks can match the four Forest Lawn establishments in size and beauty. All of them, however, impose strict control on the cemetery's appearance.

Clockwise from left:
This popular life-sized statue, known as "The Christus," was designed to rise on its pedestal above the flat landscape of the memorial park. Christ is shown releasing a bird, a symbol of the soul's resurrection, into flight; Allegheny Cemetery, Pittsburgh, Pennsylvania, 1983.

Sensuous and dramatic Pietà; Dade Memorial Park, Miami, Florida.

Fujimoto family markers; Garden of the Pines section, Evergreen Cemetery, Los Angeles, California, 1987.

Forest Lawn Memorial Park

Replica of Daniel Chester French's statue of Lincoln; Forest Lawn, Glendale, California. The original sculpture stands in Lincoln Park in Chicago. *Left*

Church of Our Heritage, "inspired by Saint George's Church in Fredericksburg, Virginia"; Forest Lawn, Colvina Hills, California. *Right*

We are very far here from the traditional conception of an adult soul naked at the judgement seat and a body turning to corruption. There is usually a marble skeleton lurking somewhere among the marble draperies and quartered escutcheons of the tombs of the high Renaissance; often you find, gruesomely portrayed, the corpse half decayed with marble worms writhing in the marble adipocere. These macaber achievements were done with a simple moral purpose—to remind a highly civilized people that beauty was skin deep and pomp was mortal. In those realistic times hell waited for the wicked and a long purgation for all but the saints, but heaven, if at last attained, was a place of perfect knowledge. In Forest Lawn, as the builder claims, these old values are reversed. The body does not decay; it lives on, more chic in death than ever before, in its indestructible Class A steel-and-concrete shelf; the soul goes straight from the Slumber Room to Paradise, where it enjoys an endless infancy.

—Evelyn Waugh, "Death in Hollywood," *Life*, 1947

Forest Lawn began as a small traditional cemetery in 1906 in Glendale, California. Only after 1917, under the direction of Hubert Eaton, "The Builder," did it become the famed memorial park that is the most visited private burial place in the United States. On New Year's Day of that year, shortly after becoming general manager of Forest Lawn, Eaton set down his future objectives. Most importantly, he argued, "the cemeteries of today are wrong because they depict an end, not a beginning. They have consequently become unsightly stoneyards, places that do nothing for humanity save a practical act, and that not too well."

After "The Builder" took charge, Forest Lawn became an assertive business organization. In a profession where others kept low profiles, Eaton was constantly in the news as he pursued his dream. On a practical level, Eaton united in one place all the diverse burial arts: undertaking, cremation, funerals, interment. The cemetery administration even controlled the style of marker that could be installed by requiring that they be purchased from the cemetery.

Borrowing the lawn park ideal from nineteenth-century administrators, Forest Lawn was the first cemetery to

This 1987 billboard for Forest Lawn Mortuaries, Glendale, California, typifies the cheerful mood that is their hallmark.

mandate the use of flat memorial tablets. The landscape itself is a Southern California version of Boston's Mount Auburn, minus the lakes and above-ground headstones. Hundreds of miles of underground pipes make verdant lawns possible, creating green hills and valleys in a place where previously only scrub and cactus grew.

Forest Lawn is pervaded by a paradoxical attempt to deal in the business of death while denying the fact of bodily decay and responding to grief's sharp pains with pleasantries of design. Like the elite rural cemeteries of the East Coast and Midwest from which it takes its clues, Forest Lawn tries to soften the idea of mortality through the use of enduring artistic styles, uplifting Christian symbolism and images identifying the cemetery with the lasting fame of the nation's heroes. Eaton distinguished the sections of the cemetery, not by numbers as was usual, but by names designed to trigger pleasant thoughts—Loving Kindness, Blessed Promise, Sheltering Hills, Abiding Love, and Enduring Faith. Comforting imagery was his trademark—a replica of Michelangelo's *David* is a recurring symbol. An elderly Los Angeles woman, visiting her husband's grave at Forest Lawn, admitted that people "pay more to be buried close to the *David*. My ten year-old grandson saw the statue and said: 'I'm glad that my grandfather is going to be protected.'" Gigantic patriotic murals, replicas of English churches and reproductions of great works of European art combine to fill the vast park-like landscape—a pruned version of "immortal nature."

With its imitation Wee Kirk o' the Heather, Duck Frog and Frog Baby statues (because "Happy innocence soothes sorrowing hearts"), chalky white "exact reproductions" of Michelangelo's sculpture, oversized copy of the gates of Buckingham Palace, and many other curiosities, Forest Lawn invites satire. Despite Forest Lawn's highly traditional combination of landscape, history, art, and Christianity, no other cemetery has been quite so eclectic in the use of symbols, exerted such total control over the look of the grounds or promoted so consistently and on such a large scale a belief in earthly good cheer in the face of death.

Ordinary Urban Cemeteries

Deserted and badly maintained, Spring Grove Cemetery in Hartford, Connecticut, has become one of the most dangerous places in the city despite its pastoral beauty. *Left*

Heavily used Fairview Cemetery, with a well-kept green lawn and large trees; Mishawaka, Indiana. *Right*

We have been to cemeteries where we have received the impression of a waffle-iron imprint pattern with some monuments dropped around here and there and a few trees thrown in for good measure.

—A.D. Taylor,
"Landscape Composition in Modern Cemetery Design,"
The American City, March 1928

Because elite garden cemeteries are more impressive and because church and country graveyards are more picturesque, the ordinary urban cemetery has been ignored by both scholars and the general public. Even people who work in them express surprise at a visitor's interest. At one in Indiana, for example, the sexton's wife interspersed her informative comments with the phrase, "that is, if you like these sorts of places."

Little documentation is available about ordinary urban cemeteries. One rarely can obtain more than a few mimeographed sheets of paper containing the date when the cemetery was established, the founders, a list of the distinguished people buried there, the total number of interments, and rules and regulations. In contrast, elite cemeteries publish elegant illustrated guides to the grounds, lists of lot owners and extended written histories.

In every aspect of the ordinary urban cemetery's physical design, economic considerations take precedence over aesthetic concerns. The city lot contains no azaleas, no rhododendrons, no Japanese maples. Instead, the original trees are left to stand, where they have not been ravaged by Dutch elm disease. The street plan tends to be similarly unimaginative and rarely follows a curvilinear path or the natural contours of the land. In crowded urban cemeteries, as the monuments tend to cover most of a family plot, a tension arises between grave markers and the natural landscape.

These "stone yards" are the nightmare of cemetery administrators who do not have the resources to repair them and who find it very difficult to maintain grounds full of headstones. Although the plots have always reflected the ethnic and religious tastes of middle and working class families, as long ago as 1900, H.A. Caparn, writing in *Park and Cemetery* magazine, described the ordinary cemeteries as "petrified forests."

Enthusiasm for urban cemeteries in the 1980s is even rarer. Whatever physical and emotional attractiveness they once had depended on the large numbers of families who regularly came and gave life to the landscape through flowers and decorations. Once the families stop visiting, the personal touch, the scrubbed look, and the feeling of human presence are gone, and the ordinary cemeteries "lose their soul."

In rows, left to right:

In this almost abandoned cemetery, angels seem to preside over the crooked markers below their tall pedestals; Baltimore Cemetery, Baltimore, Maryland, 1981.

"We are Americans and love this new country, not only with words, but with deeds, as this monument proves"; speech by Joseph Matousek, dedicating this Civil War veterans memorial; 1892, Bohemian National Cemetery, Chicago, Illinois.

Trinity Cemetery, known for its cast iron markers; Brooklyn-Queens border, New York.

Saint Raymond's Cemetery in the Bronx, with more than 5,000 burials a year, replaced Calvary in the 1980s as New York City's busiest Catholic burial ground.

At Greenwood Cemetery, small markers are set amidst trees, an arrangement rare for an ordinary cemetery south of Trenton, New Jersey; 1982.

Calvary Cemetery

Clockwise from upper right:
Recalling antique custom, funerary statues line a cemetery road.

Hundreds of life-sized marble statues in an Italian section of Calvary Cemetery.

Family markers near the heavily-used Kociuszko Bridge.

A characteristic feature of Calvary, as of all Catholic cemeteries, is the provision made for the poor and the destitute. Of the 18,275 interments in 1899, ten percent were buried in free graves.

—*Park and Cemetery*, June 1901

Calvary Cemetery in Queens, the largest American necropolis, lies within sight of the skyscrapers of midtown Manhattan. Established in 1848 as the sacred burial ground of the Roman Catholic Archdiocese of New York, by the turn of the century it handled forty-five percent of all the city's interments, and by 1989 it was the final resting place of more than two million, three hundred thousand people. Its 360 acres accommodate four times as many bodies as the more famous and more spacious Green-Wood Cemetery in nearby Brooklyn.

The graves at Calvary Cemetery record the origins and patterns of American immigration and the traditions of the Catholic church. The diverse ethnic groups are united by the myriad of sculpted crosses, saints and angels, reminders of the resurrection.

Calvary, bordering upon factories, businesses, warehouses, wide highways, and railroads, has more of a neighborhood feeling than its chaotic surroundings. The cemetery has more trees, bushes and flowers, and its human effigies stand communally in the open air, unlike the real human beings whizzing by in their vehicles. Still, at Calvary, any sense of a pastoral place of repose has been lost. Small, mass-produced stones overwhelm the plantings, dominate the grounds and turn the landscape to grey. The space, however, remains striking despite the fact that it is architecturally undistinguished; the sheer number of markers and the surrounding presence of urban life contribute to its power.

The visual stasis of row upon row of silent tombstones and the frantic agitation of the living coexist with great intensity. Unlike other cemeteries that route traffic around them, Calvary is cut by both the Brooklyn-Queens Expressway and the Long Island Expressway. Thus the monuments reverberate with the constant hum of passing vehicles, while planes taking off from nearby La Guardia Airport add to the overbearing din.

Markers, monuments and mausoleums. *Top left*

Crowded landscape of stone extending far into the distance. *Bottom left*

The Johnson mausoleum, the largest private mausoleum in the cemetery, dwarfs other tombs. *Right*

Potter's Fields

Top two rows, left to right:
Rare expression of sanctity at New York's Potter's Field, Hart Island, 1986.

Hart Island, New York, 1986.

Small temporary markers, rusted and overgrown with weeds; children's section, 1970s, Evergreen Cemetery, Camden, New Jersey.

Marker erected by a former administrator blesses the poor and declares that God made so many of them—his children—because he loved them so; Hart Island, New York, 1986.

1907, Mount Olivet Cemetery, Chicago, Illinois.

"He calleth his own by name" Hart Island, New York, 1986.

But the chief priests, taking the pieces of silver, said 'It is not lawful to put them into the treasury, since they are blood money.' So they took counsel, and bought with them the potter's field, to bury strangers in.
—*Matthew* 27: 6-7

'I don't want to go out there all by myself,' Strawberry Bill said. He had no money, and so his coffin was a box of slapsided boards and a few dozen tenpenny nails, which Francis rode with to the burial plot.... The sun then bloomed behind Francis, sending sunshine into an opening between two of the planks.... The vision stunned Francis: A great empty chasm with a dozen other coffins of crude design, similar to Bill's, piled atop one another, some on their sides, one on its end. Enough earth had been dug away to accommodate thirty or forty more such crates of the dead. In a few weeks they'd all be stacked like cordwood... 'You ain't got no worries now, Bill,' Francis told his pal. 'Plenty of company down there. You'll be lucky you get any sleep at all with them goin's on.'
—William Kennedy, *Ironweed*, 1983

Across the length and breadth of the United States, the poor are buried every day in the same impoverished circumstances that marked their earthly existence. In Camden, New Jersey, paupers are interred in unmarked plots. Those from the Chicago area are buried in groups of about thirty-five in a memorial park in Homewood. And for more than a century, the bodies of the unknown and unwanted of New York City have been ferried to Hart Island for burial in mass graves. A potter's field represents the ultimate in anonymity, a place where the names of the deceased, if known, are usually placed only on the coffins themselves. A pit is loaded with coffins until full, and the entire grave is given a single numbered marker. No friends or relations accompany the dead, and often no religious representative is on hand to perform a ceremony. Even the custom of spreading a green covering over the hole is dismissed.

Among cemeteries of this kind, New York's Potter's Field has become a space of unusual evocative power. It is on a bleak, unprepossessing island in Long Island Sound, half a mile east of the Bronx and just inside the city limits. More than 750,000 people are buried in the space of only

forty-five acres, making the ground twenty times more "crowded" than the average rural cemetery. The occasional visitor must receive special approval to enter the field and even then must approach by stages. The trip begins with a ride on a ferry carrying half a dozen soon-to-be-released convicts and a cargo of pine boxes. Once at Hart Island the "burial detail" loads the coffins onto a truck for a short trip to a seventy-five foot long trench, dug to a depth of six feet. The convicts move the coffins, scratch names on them, and shovel the dirt; guards with revolvers stand nearby. The new boxes join older ones until the trench is full; those buried last lie under only three feet of dirt. The last voyage on water, the size of the hole, the simple, uniform boxes, and the nearby presence of the ocean combine to make this an almost religious experience, although neither ceremony nor symbolism are included.

On rare occasions the body of a person previously buried in a potter' field is claimed by the family and taken to a private cemetery. In 1983, for example, an unidentified vagrant died on a subway in New York City and was buried at Potter's Field. He was identified in 1985 as a decorated World War II veteran and was reburied as a hero in 1986.

Since 1981, a Presbyterian minister has made it his duty to provide "proper burials" at the potter's field in Homewood Memorial Park, south of Chicago. Recalling that bodies used to be dumped as if they were "excess garbage" and that coffins containing human limbs were once labeled "scrap," the Reverend Joseph Ledwell reads the funeral liturgy over new arrivals from the Cook County Morgue.

Devoid of the trappings associated with an ordinary funeral, a mass burial at a potter's field is nonetheless unforgettable. Few events bring home more starkly the transitory nature of human existence, the fragility of social bonds and the power of death.

Facing page, bottom row, left to right:

Sixteen pine coffins, ready for burial at Hart Island; New York, 1986.

Convicts and coffins on the ferry to Hart Island; New York, 1986.

Coffins are buried, three deep, without ceremony or mourners; Hart Island, New York, 1986.

This page:

Metal temporary marker for an indigent child; 1976, Evergreen Cemetery, Camden, New Jersey.

THE CEMETERY AS A REFLECTION OF SOCIETY

Unlike most countries in Europe and Asia, where the citizenry has long shared a common language, religion, culture, and ethnicity, the United States has been a nation of migrants and immigrants, a place where every group is a minority. Although the country was founded under the theoretical belief that "all men are created equal," class and gender boundaries have been pervasive. As much as any other institution, the cemetery reflects the heterogeneity and variety of American life.

A Feeling of Daily Life

Charles Woolsey, a Sandy Hook pilot at the rudder of his ship; 1884, Cemetery of the Evergreens, Brooklyn, New York. *Left*

Statue of seven year-old Francesco Salerno made from the photograph at the monument's base; 1921, Mount Carmel Cemetery, Hillside, Illinois. *Right*

Let me live in a house
By the side of the road
Where the race of men go by
The men who are good
And the men who are bad
As good and as bad as I

—Epitaph, Cypress Lawn Cemetery,
Colma, California, 1975

The most striking way in which the American cemetery reflects the larger society is in the hundreds of thousands of photographic and sculpted portraits commemorating the deceased. Indeed, in quantity and breadth of representation, cemeteries offer the most comprehensive collection of American portraits from the period spanning 1880 to World War II.

As with other aspects of memorial design, portraits in exclusive rural cemeteries differ from those in ordinary burial grounds. Common throughout elite cemeteries are expensive busts, reliefs and full-length statues honoring people who played important roles in political or economic life. By contrast, sculptures of the deceased are rare in ordinary cemeteries where photographs give a human face to thousands of markers.

People portrayed as if in the midst of life constitute a widespread and striking type of funerary statuary. In cemeteries throughout America one sees images of people farming, teaching, reading a book, praying, riding a horse, or caught in the middle of a fleeting gesture. Portraits often poignantly contrast vital activity and perpetual stillness. Such statues seem to express a love for earthly existence and a desire for its continuance in the afterlife.

Clockwise from left:
Statue of Antonietta De Rosa seated between Saints Ciro and Andrew; 1932, Woodlawn Cemetery, the Bronx, New York.

Statue of thirteen year-old Mariano Raimondi, standing straight as if ready to receive instruction; 1918, Mount Carmel Cemetery, Hillside, Illinois.

Relief of a pioneer school teacher feeding the animals on her farm; 1907, Lake View Cemetery, Seattle, Washington.

Classicism in Portraiture

Bust of Emanuele Battaglini, who died in 1920 at the age of twenty-one; Holy Sepulchre Cemetery, East Orange, New Jersey. *Left*

Bust decorated with classical garland; at Oak Hill Cemetery, Washington, D.C., Eugene Liomin, "adjuster of United States standard weights and measures," is commemorated by his wife for his public service; 1862. *Right*

The memory of the just is blessed
—*Proverbs* 10: 7, Mount Auburn Cemetery, Cambridge

The American cemetery offers ordinary people the opportunity to be portrayed in a prestigious style. In the cemetery, a family or organization can bestow upon the departed the significance embodied by classicism, a significance derived from its association with monuments revering public figures.

Eyes wide open in a far-off gaze, lips firmly set, chin raised: in this mode, likenesses of ordinary people seem permanent, at peace and, in cemeteries, appropriately removed from the here-and-now. The combined naturalism

and venerability of the classical style, which both preserves and enhances memory, helped to ensure its appeal from the nineteenth century until the 1950s, when both widespread modernism and the decline of the cemetery rendered such expressions obsolete. In 1989, it was very rare for a family to commission a statue in the likeness of the deceased.

Portrait of a man in a toga; the monument is inscribed "*Sua Moglie Pose*" (erected by his wife); 1932, Holy Sepulchre Cemetery, Trenton, New Jersey. *Left*

Bust of police officer Joseph Petrosino of the New York City Police, killed in Palermo, Sicily in 1909 while investigating the Mafia; Calvary Cemetery, Queens, New York. *Center*

Life-sized granite statue in a niche sculpted with flowers, ivy and classical columns. The addition of the bleeding Sacred Heart and the cross give a Christian dimension to this otherwise worldly monument; St. Casimir Lithuanian Cemetery, Chicago, Illinois. *Right*

Righteousness Portrayed

Left to right:
Portrait of P.C. Trandberg, whose epitaph reads: "I have not shunned to declare unto you all the counsel of God (*Acts* 20:27)"; 1896, Crystal Lake Cemetery, Minneapolis, Minnesota.

Hosea Ballou, pastor of the Second Society of Universalists in Boston; 1852, Mount Auburn Cemetery, Cambridge.

Statue of the Right Reverend William Pinkney preaching; the base is inscribed: "A guileless and fearless man of God"; 1883, Oak Hill Cemetery, Washington, D.C.

We wait for peace, to no avail; for a time of healing, but terror comes instead / Jeremiah 15:19

—Epitaph for Pastor Steinle, Lutheran Cemetery, Queens, 1888

On the left is the statue of Reverend Hosea Ballou. The commemoration statue of this eminent man, who was so universally beloved and respected for his talents, his life devoted to the promulgation of the word of God, to the building up and extension of the church to which he belonged, and to the practices of all the virtues which adorn, beautify and dignify social existence, was purchased by subscriptions from the Universalist denomination at large, and was executed by Edward A. Brackett, the well-known sculptor.

—*Guide to Mount Auburn Cemetery*, 1885

The profession most frequently represented on cemetery monuments is that of the Protestant clergy. Wearing clerical garb and a stern look, ministers stand on tall shafts and look heavenward or address their congregation, now the graves arranged below them. Depicting—as in Schiller's words—"mortal vessels of truth," these monuments often include scriptural references, such as that inscribed on Queens minister Frederich Steinle's monument: "You utter what is precious, not what is worthless." Another marker, from Hartford, declares that after many years of faithful

service, the Reverend Nathan Strong was "approved and blessed by the Holy Spirit."

Statues of ministers reflect the special role of the Protestant clergy in articulating the mid-nineteenth-century concern with death, the afterlife and the cemetery. Ann Douglass, in a study of consolation literature, points out that from 1830 to 1880 liberal clergymen and devout women were "the principal authors of mourners' manuals, lachrymose verse, obituary fiction and [the popular] necrophilic biographies...." In a country undergoing rapid industrialization, both women and ministers had lost much of their status in worldly affairs. Creating a cult of death, they managed to claim a new area of influence.

Left to right:
Statue of Friederich Wilhelm Tobias Steinle, founder and First Pastor of the German Evangelistical Zions Community in Brooklyn; 1888, Lutheran Cemetery, Queens, New York.

Bronze tablet with portrait of Pastor Melchior Falk Gjertsen, donated by the Sons of Norway; 1918, Lakewood Cemetery, Minneapolis, Minnesota.

"Go ye into all the world and preach the gospel": inscription on the tombstone of William H. Rozier, "Beloved Founder and Pastor of Pleasant Hill Baptist Church"; 1937, Evergreen Cemetery, Los Angeles, California.

Photographic Portraits

Top row, left to right:
1920, Mount Carmel Cemetery, Hillside, Illinois.

Elegant studio portrait of Petras Mockus, whose life ended after eleven years; 1923, St. Casimir Lithuanian Cemetery, Chicago, Illinois.

Emma Schultz, died 1896; Concordia Lutheran Cemetery, Forest Park, Illinois.

Filomena Simak, died 1914; Bohemian National Cemetery, Chicago, Illinois.

Peter and Annie Stevens, born in Serbia in the 1870s, buried in Calvary Cemetery, Los Angeles, California, in the 1930s.

...thanks to the photograph, individual families have spontaneously found a means of imparting warmth to otherwise impersonal and unoriginal monuments....The photograph has taken the place held in major funerary art by sculpture. It speaks the same language—that of a family presence, a refusal to allow the dead to be forgotten.

—Philippe Aries, *Images of Man and Death*, 1985

A vivid human face caught in a photograph and set into carved stone personalizes a monument and reinforces a survivor's memory. Whether placed at the foot of a cross, arranged beneath an urn or a stone bible, centered on the star of David, or flanked by a dragon and a peacock, photographic portraits remind us that those depicted alive and well in the photograph are buried under our feet. On two tombstones in a section for black citizens in Evergreen Cemetery in Los Angeles, for example, portraits are placed between open gates below a dove in flight, a symbol of the departing soul.

Of all types of funerary portraits, the most common is a photograph that has been baked on enamel or porcelain and then attached to the tombstone. First originated in France in 1855, photographic portraits were common in the United States by the 1890s and, in the first decade of the new century, were advertised in Sears-Roebuck catalogues: "Imperishable Limoges porcelain portraits preserve the features of the deceased. They set firmly into the stone and remain permanent forever." The five-and-one-quarter by seven-inch portraits were billed as "a popular and appropriate manner of showing respect and affection

to a departed loved one." The prices—$11.20 for a photograph set in marble, $15.75 for one in granite—competed with the cost of many burial plots. But despite relatively high prices, hundreds of thousands of such images can be found in cemeteries all over the country.

Surprisingly, photographs more than half a century old usually exceed those of the 1980s in quality. In 1987, a Chicago memorial portrait maker, lamenting that "often the only photograph available of the deceased is one taken by a family member or from the driver's license," asserted that some images are inappropriate for display in the cemetery. In some of these pictures, for example, "people have their hair chopped off, or hold a drink in their hand or are standing on a beach wearing a bathing suit. The family wants us to put a coat and a tie on them—we can do that, and we also can remove bottles, drinks and cigarettes." Sometimes the photographs are so touched up that they resemble billboard figures.

Nonetheless, more recent photographs often show people enjoying their leisure, such as the couple in Rosedale Cemetery in New Jersey photographed on vacation in Paris with the Eiffel tower in the background or, in the same cemetery, a man and a woman snapped while drinking beer. In addition to pictures of "just folks having a good time," images of sports cars and speedboats—emblems of amusement—are sometimes engraved on the marker. Tomb photographs rendered in the familiar mode of the color snapshot may either offend or attract the visitor. Yet wherever the custom of erecting tombstones remains, a trend toward greater personalization of the marker is evident.

Facing page, bottom row, left to right:
Leo Mitlo, died 1974; Rosedale Cemetery, Linden, New Jersey.

Dianne C. Armendariz, died 1977; Holy Cross Cemetery, Los Angeles, California.

Crescent Lodge member sports group's regalia; 1982, Rosedale Cemetery, Linden, New Jersey.

Paul, died 1975; Rosedale Cemetery, Linden, New Jersey.

Eddie and wife; 1973, Rosedale Cemetery, Linden, New Jersey.

This page, clockwise from upper left:
Lucinda Walker, died 1929; Evergreen Cemetery, Los Angeles, California.

Nestor Breem, died in Meuse-Argonne, in 1920; Mount Olivet Cemetery, Chicago, Illinois.

John and Luba Mitchell, died 1965; Rosedale Cemetery, Linden, New Jersey.

Gin and Stanley, died 1979; Cypress Lawn Cemetery, Colma, California.

Ethnic Representations

Clockwise from upper left:
Russian Orthodox chapel of Saint Nicholas, 1936, and Slavic crosses; Washelli Cemetery, Seattle, Washington.

Gothic style monument of the Novotny family decorated with flower carvings and vases; 1941, Bohemian National Cemetery, Chicago, Illinois.

The benches, the bright red geraniums, the eastern European folk decorations, and the Cyrillic letters give this family monument a strong Ukranian character; Lindenwood Cemetery, Fort Wayne, Indiana.

Rest in Peace

Requiescant in Pace

Resta in Pace

Ruhe Sanft

Que en Paz Descanse

Some of the people bring their own customs and prejudices from their native country and it seems morally impossible to get them to conform to improved American ideas of cemetery management.

—Matthew P. Brazill, *Park and Cemetery*, 1912

Anxious to be buried among friends and family, immigrants give an ethnic dimension to urban cemeteries, their crowded gravestones forming neighborhoods of the dead. Monument makers trained in the "old country" retain cultural traditions, thus adding richness to otherwise ordinary cemeteries. To explain to an American monument maker what the family wants, a survivor often provides a crude drawing of a desired marker or decoration. A Chicago man, for example, remembers his father requesting a leaf design to be carved on his stone because "Germans had done this since the Middle Ages."

No bulldozing or rebuilding has been done in most of these burial places, and except for time and vandalism,

little has changed their epitaphs, photographs, carvings, and statues. Ethnic sections of cemeteries are mines of information about traditional dress, patron saints, accomplishments in life, and common symbolism.

The ubiquitous tombstone photographs of unforgettable faces, often strong and beautiful, full of energy and intelligence, remind the visitor that each grave has a unique story. General trends, such as the Americanization or assimilation of various groups, also can be traced in cemeteries. The Muller family monument in Trinity Cemetery in Manhattan bears a striking sign of the process of acculturation: the parents' inscriptions are in German, while the son anglicized his name to Miller and wrote his epitaph in English.

Still, in some cases, old world ties are so strong that an immigrant's interment takes place in the country of birth. A half-dozen funeral homes in Manhattan advertise that they can arrange to have "remains shipped worldwide." A cemetery administrator interviewed in Holland expressed familiarity with fancy American coffins, claiming that he had buried several Dutch Americans who had chosen the Netherlands as their final resting place.

Clockwise from upper left:

Chinese inscriptions and photographs in Chinese section of Rosedale Cemetery; 1946, Los Angeles, California.

A Japanese-American family's granite marker, personalized with a border of carefully chosen smooth stones; 1966, Garden of the Pines section, Evergreen Cemetery, Los Angeles, California.

Statue of a Colonel wearing his Cuban military uniform; 1972, Woodlawn Memorial Cemetery, Miami, Florida.

Italian Americans

Clockwise from left:

Photographs of sixteen members of the Mozzetti family on their tomb; 1915, Cimitero Monumentale al Verano, Rome, Italy.

Classical family monument with busts of deceased members. Statues of reverent children ornament the base; 1908, Cimitero Monumentale al Verano, Rome, Italy.

Cherub on the monument of a four year-old girl; 1907, Italian National Cemetery, Colma, California.

Small granite mausoleum of the Carrara-Marinelli family, flanked by urns and decorated with poinsettias; 1936, St. Michael's Cemetery, Stratford, Connecticut.

Dad! May God bless you on this Father's Day and safely guide you through an eternity that is filled with happiness.

—Vincent, card taped on marker,
Mount Carmel Cemetery, Hillside, 1986

In Italian sections of cemeteries one never has the feeling of being alone because hundreds of life-sized statues—looking active and engaged on their pedestals—keep a constant vigil. From the late nineteenth century until about World War II, Italian-Americans favored elaborate tomb sculptures. Over time, a family would purchase several religious statues to adorn the family plot. The most popular images were the Blessed Virgin, the Pietà, St. Joseph with the Christ Child, and angels with outspread wings, all powerful yet gentle Catholic figures. The most complex displays might include the complete Holy Family, angels, a patron saint, and a sculpted portrait. Photographs of the deceased also played an important part in articulating the monument.

As long as a feeling of kinship remained strong, the family plot was a source of comfort, pride and aesthetic satisfaction. More recently, however, Italian markers are less easily distinguished from those of other Americans.

Clockwise from left:

Crowded section of Calvary Cemetery, Queens, New York, teeming with figures in stone.

Members of the Zaccone family are interred beneath statues of the Holy Family, Christ and a female saint; 1928, Mount Carmel Cemetery, Hillside, Illinios.

Six members of the Iosco family; 1917, Mount Carmel Cemetery, Hillside, Illinois.

Family monument: *Pater familis* facing the wind atop a tall shaft; a portrait of his wife below. Calegari, a well-known turn of the century San Francisco baker, wears the plumed Italian military hat of the Bersaglieri, a special unit in World War I; Italian Cemetery, Colma, California.

The Italian Cemetery in Colma, California, with its absence of greenery and crowding of statuary is akin to European graveyards.

German Americans

Clockwise from upper left:
Lutheran Cemetery, Queens, New York.

In this group portrait of the Thiele family, the wife and child are portrayed with wings; circa 1897, Union Cemetery, Milwaukee, Wisconsin.

The sculpted trunk of a tree, a motif frequently found on German-American monuments, expresses a love of the forest. Images of hunting hounds, shotguns and a rabbit complement the emblematic shaft; Koebler monument, 1898, Lutheran Cemetery, Queens, New York.

Young woman embracing the cross; Lutheran Cemetery, Queens, New York.

The ardor with which these emigrants cherish all the ties of kin and country is well known. Far away from the homes and graveyards of their Fatherland, it is natural that they should cling together in life,—and that, in death, they should wish to lie side by side.

—Nehemiah Cleaveland, "German Lots," *Green-Wood Illustrated*, 1849

A profound sense of sadness and loss distinguishes German monuments and markers from those of other ethnic groups. The predominantly classical imagery consists of lamenting female figures, inverted torches, wreaths, urns, and perfect spheres. Carved drapery, obelisks, crosses, and the frequent use of grey granite for monuments add to the feeling of loss. While the occasional angel is more likely to join in the mourning than to point heavenward and rejoice, the life of the spirit still burns from stone lamps on the roofs of mausoleums or at the entrance to burial plots.

Nature imagery proliferates in this landscape: a profusion of sculpted leaves, branches and flowers adorn the monuments and their fences. "We Germans are romantics," said a visitor to Lutheran Cemetery in Queens, and the surrounding landscape bore him out.

The most lavish of German-American monuments are those of the great brewing magnates who first rose to prominence about a century ago. Thus the Forest Home Cemetery in Milwaukee contains the Schlitz, Pabst and Blatz monuments, while Bellefontaine Cemetery in St. Louis includes the family mausoleums of Anhauser, Busch and Wainwright, the latter designed by Louis Sullivan. These brewers, who resided in palatial residences on the most elegant streets in their cities, extended their style of life to the cemetery.

Despite the disrepair of Krueger's boarded-up downtown Newark mansion and the demolition of his brewery, this Beaux-Arts mausoleum, built in 1897 at a cost of $90,000, remains a monument to his name; Fairmont Cemetery, Newark, New Jersey. *Top left*

This unusually compact and heavy mausoleum cost the Blatz family $40,000 in 1896; Forest Home Cemetery, Milwaukee, Wisconsin. *Center*

The Wainright Mausoleum by Louis Sullivan is listed on the National Register of Historic Places; 1892, Bellefontaine Cemetery, St. Louis, Missouri. *Bottom left*

Young woman mourning against a draped, empty sofa; Dannenfelser monument, 1916, Spring Grove Cemetery, Cincinnati, Ohio. *Right*

Irish Americans

Clockwise from upper left:
Early nineteenth-century markers like these, the writing deeply engraved into the stone, are the pride of the caretaker at Old Brook Cemetery, Dublin, Ireland.

Deathbed scene on James Hegan's marker, erected by his sister Bridget; 1856, Holy Cross Cemetery, Brooklyn, New York.

Classical mourning relief with Christian symbols; 1871, Holy Cross Cemetery, Brooklyn, New York.

Mary Nichols is my name
Ireland is my nation
Catholic Church is my belief
Heaven is my expectation

—Epitaph, New Orleans cemetery

Holy Cross Cemetery, one of the oldest and largest predominantly Irish-Catholic cemeteries in the country, is rich in mid-nineteenth-century Irish markers. Established in 1849 in the town of Flatbush, Brooklyn, in 1989 Holy Cross held more than a half-million entombments in its one hundred acres of land. In the earliest section of the cemetery, hundreds of tombstones display traditional Hibernian motifs.

In nineteenth-century Ireland, the typical grave marker was a simple stone slab, often shaped like an arched portal. In addition to bearing the deceased's name and a religious image, it was inscribed with carefully lettered information: dates of birth and death, the name and relationship of the person who erected the marker, and sometimes even the former street address and career of the deceased. In the United States, the format continued, and many immigrants added to the monument their county and parish of birth and an epitaph. For economic reasons,

Irish-American markers from the first wave of immigration were usually narrower than those in the old country. Made of marble, with shallow carving, most of these modest markers have lost their inscriptions to erosion.

Although the Irish "do not go for statues as Italians do," their strong Catholic faith is occasionally expressed in life-sized renderings of a narrow range of subjects: particularly the Virgin Mary and the free-standing cross. Surprisingly, St. Patrick, patron saint of Ireland, is rarely seen. Most crosses bear the monogram IHS, "Jesus, savior of mankind," and many are of the Celtic type. Sculpted reliefs illustrate the Resurrection, the Virgin Mary, the face of Christ, the Crucifix, and the sacrificial lamb on an altar. Deathbed scenes do not describe death as the end: angels perch on the clouds awaiting the deceased's entry into paradise.

In early memorials, religion formed an essential theme, with personal feelings rarely expressed. Except for biographical information, nothing addressed the deceased as an individual. In the late nineteenth century the symbols and forms of inscription of the earliest markers remained, but Irish-American monuments became larger, more expensive and more distinctively individualistic. In St. Patrick's Cemetery in Hartford, the monuments grew to be nearly indistinguishable from those in the adjacent elite Old North Cemetery. A Catholic priest in Hartford explained the similarity by saying: "Old Yanks here were looked upon as symbols of success."

Perhaps because of their aesthetic appeal, Celtic crosses later became popular among Americans of many ethnic origins. Shortly after World War I, for example, the Sears-Roebuck Catalogue offered a seven-foot model for $290 and an impressive ten-foot version for $584. These prices represented significant financial commitments, being comparable to those for automobiles at that time.

Clockwise from left:

Ornate Celtic cross on the grave of the Right Reverend Charles McCready; Calvary Cemetery, Queens, New York.

A tall, unusually refined figure of Christ, erected on Thomas Keegan's grave by his wife; Old Brook Cemetery, Dublin, Ireland.

Shafts supporting statues of the Blessed Virgin; Saint Peter's Cemetery, Jersey City, New Jersey.

A brown stone obelisk, like those of the "old Yanks" buried nearby, combines images of the cross and the deceased's county of origin in Ireland; 1862, St. Patrick's Cemetery, Hartford, Connecticut.

Jewish Americans

Jewish section, separated by tall poplars from the rest of Washelli Cemetery; Seattle, Washington. *Left*

Blessing hands, associated with the Cohen family; circa 1890, Oak Park Cemetery, Ligonier, Indiana. *Right*

Then shall the dust return to the earth as it was; and the spirit shall return unto god who gave it.

—*Ecclesiastes* 12: 7

Jewish law prescribes funerary rituals in detail, including the design and layout of cemeteries and the distance at which bodies must be separated from each other and from Gentiles. For instance, Orthodox Jews must be buried in consecrated ground within twenty-four hours of death, but if interment would then take place on the Sabbath, it must be postponed until the following day.

To secure and consecrate a burial place was a primary concern of the Jewish-American community in the nineteenth century. Satisfying this need even preceded the choice of a place of worship. According to historian H. Grinstin, synagogues controlled and owned the Jewish cemeteries until the middle of the last century; afterwards, independent mutual aid societies (*landsmanschaften*) began to own cemetery plots and take complete charge of all funeral arrangements.

As was the case with cemetery organizations of other immigrant groups, Jewish mutual aid societies, especially those of eastern Europeans, flourished in the first half of the twentieth century. Many of their burial grounds occupied small fenced-off sections of much larger non-denominational cemeteries, and graves, like those in old

church graveyards, were arranged in the order in which members died rather than according to family groups. Because most eastern European arrivals were poor, and their burial societies could not afford to reserve land for the pastoral ideals of elite cemeteries, literally every inch of the space was taken up by graves. As historian Michael Weisser has observed, the burial areas lack walkways, space between monuments or headstones, landscaping, benches, and other ornamental features. The headstones are engraved in Hebrew or Yiddish, and many are without dates. Often it is difficult to tell where the burial plot of one society ends and another begins.

Assimilated and wealthy native-born Jews of northern European origin were buried in large elite cemeteries, such as Salem Fields in Brooklyn, established in the 1850s. The monuments in these cemeteries have a strong German influence, with a classicizing stamp, and are similar in size and design to the markers of all denominations in rural cemeteries.

In more recent Jewish cemeteries where most monuments date from the 1930s or later, popular motifs include tree-trunks with truncated branches, lions, the Star of David, the two tablets of the law, candlesticks (evocative of the human spirit), and emblems of professions. Blessing hands, a common symbol of the clergy, are often seen on the tombs of people whose surnames derive from Cohen; of the twelve tribes of Israel, the Kahans were the priests. The grave markers of the earlier immigrants, by contrast, are simple, unadorned slabs.

In rows, left to right:

Rough stone remains on the reverse of many monuments; circa 1930s, Mount Judah Cemetery, Queens, New York.

Entrance to Mount Judah Cemetery. The names of the cemetery organizers are written on the stone pillars; 1921, Queens, New York.

Jewish cemetery, next to a brewery; Newark, New Jersey, 1981.

Recent graves of Russian Jews, the markers decorated with flowers, photographs and religious symbols; Hollywood Memorial Cemetery, Los Angeles, California.

Crowded Jewish section within Oak Woods Cemetery; Chicago, Illinois.

Detail of marker with photograph and Star of David; circa 1930s, Goule Chesed Shel Cemetery, Hillside, Illinois.

Hispanic Americans

Open gates of heaven reveal a dark-skinned Christ crowned by thorns. The colors were applied through the lithochrome technique; 1982, Saint Raymond's Cemetery, the Bronx, New York.

Septiembre 17, 1932
Murio Eusebio Gallegos
—Marker inscription, eastern New Mexico

The Spanish presence in America dates from the sixteenth century, especially in the pueblos and missions of the southwest, yet few signs of early burial practices remain. Since the 1950s, however, the Hispanic population of the country's largest cities has grown rapidly, and today their graves are among the most common in the newer sections of Catholic cemeteries. Although Hispanics do not belong to a single nationality, they all share "a great respect for the dead," according to a New York undertaker.

The grave markers of the most numerous Hispanic groups in the United States—Mexicans, Puerto-Ricans and Cubans—frequently include crosses, the face of Christ, a pair of praying hands, patron saints, or—most importantly—the Virgin Mary. Mexicans prefer statues and even stickers of the brown-skinned Virgin of Guadalupe on their monuments; Cubans favor images of "La Virgen de la Caridad del Cobre," the Virgin as she appeared to three fisherman in a boat off the Cuban province of El Cobre; Puerto-Ricans request "La Milagrosa"—Mary as miracle-worker, standing on a globe with her arms reaching out toward the viewer, light radiating from her hands and a snake—a symbol of evil—crushed under her feet.

The most common offerings to the dead are flowers. As a Puerto-Rican mourner in Miami noted, "My father, before he died, selected the flowers he wanted placed on his grave, and he planted them in the garden. Now that he is dead we do not let the flowers on his tomb get dry." An undertaker from Manhattan, where gardens are rare, remarked that Hispanics "throw away too much money on flowers." Hispanics favor candles as well. For Puerto-Ricans, according to a monument salesman in New Jersey, "a candle lights the path through darkness."

Monument dealers expect a long-term relationship with Hispanic families. The initial sale is of a "small, medium, or elegant" stone, a $1000-plus "one-time item that will last forever." The cost of the foundation and installation, not to mention sculpted images or additional inscriptions, can add hundreds of dollars to the expense. Later, the family may "give the deceased a birthday present"—for example, a porcelain portrait at a cost of between $125 and $200, so that the family can "see the deceased when they go visit the cemetery." For other holidays, such as Mother's Day, the survivors may buy a vigil candle that burns for a week for $50 (refills, $3.50) or simply a card.

When additional members of the family die, the monument maker will write the new name on the stone for a fee or sell another monument to the family if the grave is full. The monument maker's services include coloring the stone ("lithochrome"), a practice added after families themselves initiated it, painting the gray surface of their family markers with bright yellows, greens, reds and blue. The effort and expense that Hispanics tend to incur for the commemoration of their dead represents more than a survival of ancestral burial customs; it signifies a claim to their adopted land as well.

Clockwise from left:

Virgen de la Caridad del Cobre protecting the helpless fishermen on a stormy sea; Woodlawn Memorial Cemetery, Miami, Florida, 1984.

Marker topped by a statue of the Virgen de Guadalupe, patron saint of Mexico; Mount Olivet Cemetery, Denver, Colorado.

Flowers, greeting cards and perpetual candle suggest the importance attached to this grave; 1986, Saint Raymond's Cemetery, the Bronx, New York.

Cheerful floral arrangement on parents' grave; Catholic Cemetery, Fort Wayne, Indiana.

The Sandoval family continues to address their father by taping cards and photographs to his tombstone; 1981, Mount Olivet Cemetery, Denver, Colorado.

Tile image of Our Lady of Guadalupe presides over Mexican-American section of Calvary Cemetery, Los Angeles, California.

Family Plots

Clockwise from upper left:
Harris family plot; 1860s, Mount Auburn Cemetery, Cambridge, Massachusetts.

Laurel Hill Cemetery, Philadelphia.

Kunhardt family plot, headstones leading up to a portico inscribed with: "They rest from their labors, their works do follow them"; Moravian Cemetery, Staten Island, New York.

Large Victorian figural group known as "The Three Sisters"; circa 1908, Cedar Lawn Cemetery, Paterson, New Jersey.

Individualized monuments and markers decorate the Whitlock family plot; Green-Wood Cemetery, Brooklyn, New York.

It is the ambition of the New Yorker to live upon the Fifth Avenue, to take his airings in the Park, and to sleep with his fathers in Green-Wood.

—*The New York Times*, March 30, 1866

The burial plots of extended families and of occupational groups reveal broad social patterns. Older graveyards reflect the beliefs of generations, their family relationships and their affiliations; for immigrants, cemeteries fostered a sense of identity and stability in a new country characterized by change. Today many associations once represented in burial grounds have disappeared.

Family monuments and plots with as many as thirty separate spaces remain commonplace. In pre-World War II cemeteries, several generations were often buried together, with each member's space designated by a small marker grouped before a large family monument. A typical family plot was referred to by the surname of the family that owned it, and its graves were arranged according to the status and order of burial of the individual members. At less expansive urban cemeteries, several family members were generally buried on a smaller plot marked by a single monument, their names crowded together on its face and continuing on the sides and the back when necessary.

Before the 1850s, family plots were commonly demarcated by iron fences which, according to historian Stanley French, "served little practical purpose in the well supervised rural cemetery." He quotes a pair of visitors to Mount Auburn in the 1850s: "The elegant iron rails which divide the small lots, are neither ornamental nor...reverential for the place. Exclusiveness little befits a cemetery; the idea of private property, carried even into the realm of the dead, where no one can own more than he covers, has something unnaturally strange." The unity of the landscape was broken by the rails, and the practice made upkeep much more expensive.

In the last decades of the nineteenth century, following the lead of Spring Grove Cemetery in Cincinnati, administrators sought to eliminate large, distinctive, fenced family plots. Instead of wrought iron barriers, they encouraged the practice of setting the monument back from the cemetery street. Efficiency eventually prevailed over the wishes of families, and the fences, images of both exclusivity and family unity, were removed.

Clockwise from upper left:

Hearts and crosses, symbols of love and Christianity, decorate the marker of two sisters; 1970, Cypress Lawn Cemetery, Colma, California.

The death of a child prompted a farm family to erect a marker with both the name of the deceased child and those of the living parents; 1982, Sparta Cemetery, Kimmel, Indiana.

On an Austrian-American family plot, a tall column topped by a playful sculpted cherub; 1913, Lutheran Cemetery, Queens, New York.

Merriman family plot with fifteen markers around a monumental shaft; 1860s, Riverside Cemetery, Waterbury, Connecticut.

Vanderbilt Family Cemetery

Clockwise from upper left:
Massive arched cemetery entrance.

Polished marble tombs of Vanderbilt family members; circa 1895.

White marble sarcophagi of Edith Sheppard Fabri (died 1954) and her young son, Ernesto Giusepe (died 1909). His inscription reads: "It is not the will of your father which is in heaven that one of these little ones should perish, *Matthew* 18-44."

These are not weak imitations, pretentious and futile attempts, such as in every country bring ridicule upon braggarts and upstarts. No. In every detail and finish they reveal conscientious style, technical care. Evidently the best artist has been chosen, and he has had both freedom and money. Especially money.

—Paul Bourget, on the palaces by Richard Morris Hunt for the Vanderbilt family, circa 1890

The permanently closed, tall iron gates and the stone archway leading to the Vanderbilt Cemetery are located within the grounds of Moravian Cemetery in New Dorp, Staten Island, the village where Commodore Cornelius Vanderbilt grew up. The visitor to Moravian Cemetery who ventures through the south perimeter faces an entrance to an important yet unnamed destination. A paved road through thickly planted fir trees poses a challenge to explore what lies beyond.

The road winds uphill amidst thick greenery. After a hundred yard ascent to one of the highest points on the island, a clearing on the left is revealed, and against a backdrop of trees, one sees a light grey medieval chapel made of Quincy granite, the largest private mausoleum in America.

Vanderbilt mausoleum, modelled after the twelfth-century church of St. Gilles, near Arles, France; Richard Morris Hunt, architect, 1886.

The Vanderbilt mausoleum, designed by Richard Morris Hunt, was completed in 1886. William H. Vanderbilt commissioned Hunt to build a "roomy, solid and rich" mausoleum "appropriate to the family fortunes." Since he feared theft of the family remains, as had happened in the cases of Abraham Lincoln and the financier A.T. Stewart, Vanderbilt also demanded a secure facility. Known as "The Vanderbilt Family Architect," Hunt, trained at the Beaux Arts school in Paris, found in French architecture the models with which to please American millionaires. He designed the Vanderbilt mausoleum after the twelfth-century chapel of St. Gilles in Arles, France.

Twenty-six Vanderbilts are buried in the mausoleum. Broad steps lead to three large arched portals within an intricately patterned facade. The original stained-glass windows have been removed, however, and the openings sealed. The twenty-two acres of grounds, landscaped by Frederick Law Olmsted, once offered visitors views of the New York Bay, now blocked by tall trees. Plenty of cleared land is still left for burials and for other mausoleums. But more than a century after its completion, the Vanderbilt mausoleum is no longer important to newer generations of the family, and the site itself is not well-kept. The most frequent visitors are adventurous teenagers who penetrate the massive gates and fences to drink and make love under great trees overlooking the ocean, amidst funerary monuments fit for royalty.

Monuments to Marriage

Clockwise from upper left:
Twin markers, similar to those found in colonial graveyards; 1891, Mount Auburn Cemetery, Cambridge, Massachusetts.

Simple stone with image of a bungalow inscribed, "Our Home"; 1941, Montesano plot, Oak Ridge Cemetery, Hillside, Illinois.

Figures of Augusta and Carl Niss repose like *gisants* (recumbent effigies) on a medieval tomb; 1905, Union Cemetery, Milwaukee, Wisconsin.

Intimate bronze statues of the Kurgonais sculpted by their son; 1984, St. Casimir Lithuanian Cemetery, Chicago, Illinois.

Marker of a Polish-American couple; 1905, All Souls Polish Cemetery, Chicago, Illinois.

Nor time nor death shall ever part them more.
—Richard Blair, "The Grave," 1743

The family bond most often celebrated in cemeteries is that of husband and wife. Unlike other themes of funerary art, the marriage connection is commemorated by every ethnic group, occupation, class, and race. A shared marker commonly includes the names of a man and a woman side by side, often with the designation "husband" and "wife" or "father" and "mother." Similarly, the doubling of motifs —urns, fronds, headstones—concisely and pervasively conveys the concept of marriage, as does the inclusion of wedding portraits or the engraving of the wedding date inside bells, rings or hearts.

Such representations of the bonds of marriage are among the most striking examples of funerary art. For example, the sculpture of a recumbent couple (Carl and

Augusta Niss) of about 1905 is an extraordinary monument in the otherwise ordinary Union Cemetery, Milwaukee. Rendered in a royal manner, these full-length portraits attract many visitors who have been "guided to them by word of mouth." Less spectacular, but with a similar feeling of perpetual togetherness, are the busts of another German-American couple in Denver's Fairmount Cemetery. Under the sheltering roof of their classical monument, likenesses of man and wife have been facing each other for three-quarters of a century.

The grave marker of the Montesanos—which includes the outline of a typical Chicago bungalow and the engraved words "Our Home"—plays on the idea of the grave as a residence. Unlike some of its Victorian equivalents, this simple marker shows a preference for the former earthly dwelling. In this instance the husband's side of the stone is distinguished from his wife's by the addition of a cross. Likewise, on a monument for Governor Hamilton Rowan Gamble and his wife Mary (both died 1864), the husband's truncated obelisk is taller than his companion's, to which it is nevertheless linked by a garland of flowers. Despite these isolated variations, on most American marriage monuments the notion of equality is conveyed.

Governor Gamble and wife; 1864, Bellefontaine Cemetery, St. Louis, Missouri. *Left*

1880, Spring Grove Cemetery, Cincinnati, Ohio. *Center*

Griffith monument depicting Charles and wife Jane in front of their Brooklyn house on the day of her death; 1857, Green-Wood Cemetery, Brooklyn, New York. *Top right*

White marble busts of Frank and Bette Kaub facing each other inside a house-shaped monument; 1911, Fairmount Cemetery, Denver, Colorado. *Bottom right*

Memorials to Children

Clockwise from upper left:
Sleep, a reassuring symbol of death, and the tragic reality of a child in his coffin coexist in this grave monument. Marker is inscribed in Italian, "The afflicted parents"; 1919, Italian Cemetery, Colma, California.

Cypress Lawn Cemetery, Colma, California.

1926, Fairmount Cemetery, Denver, Colorado.

Eroded moss-covered statue of a lively looking child; Spring Grove Cemetery, Cincinnati, Ohio.

"Baby Joe"; Mount Pleasant Cemetery, Newark, New Jersey.

"One sufferer on earth/And an angel in heaven"; 1865, Spring Grove Cemetery, Cincinnati, Ohio.

A precious one from us has gone,
A voice we loved is stilled,
A place is vacant in our home,
Which never can be filled.

—Epitaph for Lillian Maud Thomson, age five,
Forest Hills Cemetery, Duluth, Minnesota, 1899

During the nineteenth century as much as 40 percent of the total death rate was comprised of the death of children under the age of five. Not until the turn of the twentieth century, with improvements in public health, nutrition, and general standard of living, was there a dramatic downturn in the infant death rate.

—Nancy Schrom Dye and Daniel Blake Smith,
"Mother Love and Infant Death, 1750–1920,"
Journal of American History, 1986

The death of a child is an event for which no one can ever be prepared. The fear of such a devastating moment lurks in the heart of every parent; its realization is a living nightmare. Mourning the death of a parent is comparatively easy because to a child, the parent is the past, while to a parent the child is the future. When the young are taken, mourning is never completed, and grief is a companion for life.

Not surprisingly, life-sized sculptures of infants and small children constitute a popular motif in cemeteries. Depicted as vulnerable, their bodies barely covered, these sentimental images address the pedestrian as well as the heavens. Portrayals of infants are not likenesses; identical sculptures of babies in sleeping gowns can be found on different graves. On the other hand, children over the age of five are usually portrayed as unique individuals. Not only faces, but clothes are particularized: the carving of boots, bows, lace collars, cuffs, and in some cases even jewelry demonstrates that these were expensive statues requiring careful craftsmanship. Some children carry

blossoms and wreaths, others small luxuries: an elegant girl holds a parasol, a beautifully groomed boy has a lace handkerchief in his small hand, and another boy, serious and sad, unfurls a scroll inscribed with his name and that of his parents.

Portraits of children, hauntingly posing the mystery of their brief existence, are among the most compelling funerary statues; visitors frequently place flowers in their hands. Magazine articles on cemeteries often include such statues among the illustrations. Unfortunately, images of deceased children—like revered works of art—also attract vandals, who break off limbs, smash faces or knock the statues from their pedestals. In Calvary Cemetery in Evanston, Illinois, the marble statue of eleven year-old Josie, who died in 1891, was toppled so many times that the family encased it in plexiglass. Vandals continued to knock down the figure and roll it along the cemetery streets. Still, today, almost a century after the child's death, descendants are willing to spend the money necessary to insure that the monument, and this image of their ancestral heritage and family name, survives.

Clockwise from left:

"Willie, Mary, and Charlie"; 1856, Mount Auburn Cemetery, Cambridge, Massachusetts.

Monument commemorating a boy who died at the age of 12; 1881, Gardens of Memories Cemetery, Salinas, California.

Lars and Ruth Schmidt; 1890s, Waldheim Cemetery, Forest Park, Illinois.

1926, Lutheran Cemetery, Queens, New York.

Seated statue of fashionably dressed seven year-old girl; 1880, Graceland Cemetery, Chicago, Illinois.

1888, Lakewood Cemetery, Minneapolis, Minnesota.

Willie Roemer, age seven; 1902, Waldheim Cemetery, Forest Park, Illinois.

Plots for Organizations

Clockwise from upper left:
Tall obelisk marking the Actors Fund of America plot for indigent thespians; Kensico Cemetery, Valhalla, New York.

The graves of Catholic bishops, priests and nuns; Calvary Cemetery, St. Paul, Minnesota.

Markers inscribed with the rank of the deceased; Salvation Army plot, Kensico Cemetery, Valhalla, New York.

White crosses of the Sisters of Mercy; Holy Cross Cemetery, Colma, California.

A plot of ground laid off in the form of three concentric circles is... planned for the new addition to Mount Olivet Cemetery, Dubuque, Ia.... In the center it is the intention to erect a chapel or a large monument. The inner circle...will be the burial place for bishops and archbishops. The second circle will be the resting place of priests and the outer one will be reserved for sisters of the various religious orders....
—*Park and Cemetery*, May 1903

The employees of Lake Erie and Western R. R., have raised a fund for the purchase of...ground for a cemetery...for the interment of dead railroaders whose bodies are not claimed by friends.... Funds have also been raised to defray other funeral expenses....
—*Park and Cemetery*, December 1898

Promoted to higher service.
—Epitaph for Major Hilda Freed, Salvation Army plot, Oak Ridge Lutheran Cemetery, Hillside, Illinois, 1939

Some organizations, particularly those with a family character, maintain their own plots in American cemeteries. Many professional groups—including those of actors, circus performers, seamen, and railroad workers—traditionally have made provisions for the burial of members who die indigent. At The Evergreens Cemetery in Brooklyn, the Actors Fund of America dedicated a plot in 1887 to the burial of its members. The same cemetery has a three-acre area belonging to the Seamen's Cemetery Association, for merchant sailors from any nation who die in New York; many of these men otherwise would have been buried at Potter's Field. The seamen's plot, established in the mid-nineteenth century, is graced by a large monument with a globe, symbolizing "voyagers of the earth."

The Evergreens Cemetery also contains two late nineteenth-century statues commemorating fire fighters who lost their lives in the line of duty. One statue shows a fireman with a hand on a hydrant. The other figure carries a small child in bed clothes to safety. In Newark's Mount Pleasant Cemetery, old-fashioned fire hydrants fence a firemen's plot; at the center a figure looks up, indicating the route to heaven with a raised hand.

The Salvation Army has plots for its officers in cemeteries in Valhalla, New York; Westchester, Illinois; Atlanta, Georgia; and Los Angeles, California. Every year on Memorial Day members participate in a special service. The ceremony begins with the placement of the Salvation Army flag on the graves of the dead members, continues with the announcement of the names of those who died during the last year and ends with the sounding of taps.

Catholic cemeteries devote special sections to members of the clergy. In Calvary Cemetery in St. Paul, members of religious orders are buried next to the tombs of their bishops. The markers on the bishops' graves are flat, like the floor slabs in a cathedral where bishops are more often buried. The arrangement is hierarchical, with priests buried closest to the bishops and the Sisters of the Poor—represented by tiny, cement crosses—farthest away. Although the majority of those interred were immigrants from France, Ireland, Germany, and Spain who came to Minnesota as adults, the diversity of national origin is not readily apparent in the almost military order of the monuments.

Clockwise from upper left:
Burial ground of the Society of Jesus. A life-sized sculptural group of the Crucifixion dominates the large circular plot separated from the rest of the cemetery by paved roads; Holy Name Cemetery, Jersey City, New Jersey.

Firemen's plots, with fence posts in the form of old-fashioned fire hydrants, surround an elevated statue of one of their members; Mount Pleasant Cemetery, Newark, New Jersey.

High on a pedestal inscribed with the words"Fidelity" and "Brotherly Love," a bronze elk marks the plot of the Fraternal Order of the Elks; Mountain View Cemetery, Oakland, California.

Circus animals lined up as if to perform; Miami Showmen's Association section of Southern Memorial Park, Miami, Florida.

DESIGNING FOR ETERNITY

More than any place other than a house of God, a cemetery reminds us of the age-old quest for eternal life. Even before Christianity, humans found solace in the belief of an after-life, that is—in an eternity. Plato noted that many a man had gone willingly to the world below with the hope of seeing there a deceased wife or son.

The great age of American cemetery art spanned the years 1850 to 1930. Families designed and decorated their plots to express the ideals of their class or, simply, according to personal whim. Hoping their personal monuments would last as long as ancient models, wealthy families built reduced versions of the pyramids, the Parthenon, medieval cathedrals, and other historical landmarks. Many spent $10,000 or more for the building alone.

At the other extreme, those who rejected classical authority made markers of nature's strong unpolished forms. Glacial boulders, which bear witness to the frontier spirit of the country, were considered uniquely American monuments. At the turn of this century, Kansas Senator John J. Ingalls wrote, "I hate these obelisks, urns and stone cottages, and should prefer a great natural rock…one of the great boulders known as the 'last rocks' of the prairie…with a small surface smoothed down, just large enough to make a tablet in which could be inserted the bronze letters of our name, Ingalls, and nothing else."

Cemetery Entrances

Clockwise from left:

"Norman" towers flank the entrance to Cypress Lawn Cemetery; Colma, California.

Gothic entrance of 1877 with its three pointed arches frames the ordinary buildings of the surrounding area; Mount Pleasant Cemetery, Newark, New Jersey.

1797 entrance to Mision de San Miguel, central California, grave site of over two thousand Indians.

Entrance from A.W.N. Pugin's *An Apology for the Revival of Christian Architecture in England* (1843). This cemetery gate reflects Pugin's support of the spirit and forms of medieval Christianity in face of the blatantly pagan and commercial mixtures of Classical and Egyptian styles then popular.

The threshold is the limit, the boundary, the frontier that distinguishes and opposes two worlds—and at the same time the paradoxical place where those worlds communicate, where passage from the profane to the sacred world becomes possible.

—Mircea Eliade, *The Sacred and the Profane*, 1957

Nothing adds more to the dignity and impressiveness of a park or cemetery than an artistic entrance.

—*Park and Cemetery*, July 1915

Cemetery entrances, whether simple or grandiose, break the continuity of the surrounding neighborhood and announce a special realm dedicated to the departed. Massive entrances, set against a landscape and ornamented with turrets, spires or columns, were designed to be noted by the slow corteges of the pre-automobile era, when a funeral could last an entire day. Although in our age of quick transportation few travelers and visitors appreciate these monumental gateways, processions still routinely block traffic on their way to the grave.

In the early twentieth century, commercial considerations overwhelmed commemorative ones. Impressive entrances made the cemetery more desirable, dignified and exclusive. In dozens of articles and illustrations from the first decade of the twentieth century, *Park and Cemetery* stressed the need for durable, artistic entrances that would provide "a pleasing introduction to the beautiful grounds." Gateways lent "an air of exclusiveness...that to most of us, is distinctly desirable." The appeal to status found its corollary in the advertisements of gate manufacturers, who billed their products as equally appropriate for parks, estates or cemeteries.

A variety of symbols enhance the architectural grandeur of typical entrances. The gates of Brooklyn's Green-Wood Cemetery form the shape of a cathedral facade, complete with sculpted reliefs of Christ raising the dead. Monumental eagles gaze down over the entrance to Arlington National Cemetery, while royal lions—generic symbols of rank and prestige—adorn the gates to non-denominational Forest Lawn in Glendale, California. And throughout the land, the cross of Jesus is ubiquitous at cemetery entrances. Whether their style and conception are sacred or profane, gateways are essential in denoting and dignifying the passage between the world of the living and the domain of the dead.

In addition to indicating passage or an abstract sense of security, the elaborate gates and fences of cemeteries serve a practical function in regulating visitation and preserving the sanctity and physical integrity of the cemetery. Although most Americans avoid burial places even during the day, certain citizens are especially drawn to cemeteries after dark. These nocturnal intruders include thieves who wish to remove stained glass, other expensive objects or even from bodies themselves from mausolea, couples who can find no other place for intimacy, teenagers who experience a temporary thrill when they knock over an upright monument, and members of religious cults who engage in animal sacrifice and other voodoo rituals. The impregnability implied by the century-old entrances has become a functional requirement given the strains of modern society.

Clockwise from upper left:
Heavy iron fence and gates, next to soaring Gothic tower; Penn Avenue Gate, 1888, Allegheny Cemetery, Pittsburgh, Pennsylvania.

This extraordinary Gothic entrance, now a ruin, is an unexpected "Old World" sight in the Central Ward of Newark, New Jersey. The bell tower and guard house has lost its gates and now stands as a picturesque monument without a function; Woodland Cemetery, 1988.

Massive castellated entrance; Baltimore Cemetery, Baltimore, Maryland.

The quality of this entryway to Woodland Cemetery prepares the visitor for the profusion of well-designed monuments inside; Cleveland, Ohio.

Classical Revivals

Clockwise from upper left:
The Lowry Goodrich mausoleum, modeled after the Parthenon, on a hilltop in Lakewood Cemetery, Minneapolis, Minnesota.

The refined Greek Revival mausoleum of Alice Hastings Minot in the Santa Barbara Cemetery enjoys a particularly lovely site by the Pacific Ocean; 1954, Santa Barbara, California.

The Greek Revival monuments in this section of Allegheny Cemetery in Pittsburgh, Pennsylvania create the feeling of an ancient landscape, despite the fact that the tombs are only sixty years old.

Not magnitude, not lavishness,
But Form—the Site;
Not innovating wilfulness,
But reverence for the Archetype.
—Herman Melville, "Greek Architecture," 1891

The Grogan Parthenon reminded Francis of something, but he could not say what. He stared at it and wondered, apart from its size, what it signified. He knew nothing of the Acropolis, and little more about Grogan except that he was a rich and powerful Albany Irishman whose name everybody used to know. Francis could not suppose that such a massive marbling of old bones was a sweet conflation of ancient culture, modern coin, and self-apotheosis.

—William Kennedy, *Ironweed*, 1983

In American cemeteries, the most popular revival style is the classical, with its vocabulary of columns, pediments and idealized, well-proportioned figures. J.N.B. DePouilly, a French architect who came to Louisiana in the 1830s with scale drawings of the best-known monuments of Père-Lachaise, built at Saint Louis Cemeteries in New Orleans some of the earliest American examples of the Classical Revival. The classical style became an early favorite in New Haven's Grove Street Cemetery, in Cambridge's Mount Auburn and in mid-nineteenth-century burial grounds throughout the Northeast.

Classical designs were criticized by Christians who expected funerary monuments to reflect a belief in resurrection and the afterlife. Nehemiah Cleaveland wrote in 1849 that the Greek style was inappropriate in America: "No one can doubt that in their own time and place, these symbols were natural and appropriate, as well as beautiful. But are they so still? Seen among the cypress of an Ionian cemetery, or over the ashes of some beloved and lamented Athenian youth, the fragmentary column, or the torch reversed and going out in darkness, was a fit expression of the popular belief, and truly symbolized a sorrow in which hope had neither lot nor part: To the mourners of pagan antiquity, death was extinction."

White granite memorial for Mary Baker Eddy and her husband, designed by Egerton Swartout and built at a cost of $110,000. The circular colonnade, open to the sky, sports red plantings at its center; 1915, Mount Auburn Cemetery, Cambridge, Massachusetts. *Left*

Grunow Mausoleum, 1920s, Forest Home Cemetery, Hillside, Illinois. The cemetery administrator reported: "Grunow was an industrialist; he started a company in Chicago called Majestic Radio. He made a lot of money and wanted to show something for it—like, he lived in a big house." *Top right*

Duda family mausoleum; Bohemian National Cemetery, Chicago, Illinois. *Bottom right*

Islet with William A. Clark mausoleum. Known as the copper king of Montana and Arizona, Clark was also a United States Senator; 1925, Hollywood Memorial Cemetery, Los Angeles, California.

Despite such objections, many wealthy Americans adopted the Greek style for their final resting place. Thirteen out of twenty-nine monuments selected by the *Architectural Record* in 1900 to illustrate "How the Rich are Buried" embodied clearly classical conventions, and two others included strong classical elements. Similarly, *Park and Cemetery* noted at the turn of the century that the Greek and Roman styles represented "the better class of monuments," and the magazine encouraged cemetery administrators to save their best locations by lakes or on hills for imposing examples. Standing in isolation, these monuments imitated those in the paintings of Claude Lorrain.

Greek and Roman monuments could easily cost tens of thousands of dollars and require materials and talented craftsmen from several cities at home and abroad. With these structures wealthy families sought to enrich the cultural life of their communities as well as to link their names to the masterpieces that were otherwise inaccessible to most ordinary citizens. Thus, J.H. Wade, who built a memorial chapel in Cleveland's Lake View

Cemetery, reportedly "raised a temple to art the like of which few communities have to show" (*Park and Cemetery*, 1903). Other highly praised monuments include copies of Scipio's tomb (Forest Home, Milwaukee), the Parthenon (Lakewood, Minneapolis), and the temple of Theseus (Woodlawn, New York City).

As with other revival styles, classicism continued to inspire designs for almost a century. After the Depression, however, ostentatious funerary monuments were rarely built.

Feigenspan monument, circa 1920, Fairmount Cemetery, Newark, New Jersey. *Top left*

Detached classical portal with Crucifixion scene and a color photograph of the deceased couple at center; 1970s, New Calvary Cemetery, Los Angeles, California. *Bottom left*

Section of a Greek Revival monument depicting a family gathering about a table; late 1890s, Calvary Cemetery, Queens, New York. *Center*

Row of mausoleums; Allegheny Cemetery, Pittsburgh, Pennsylvania. *Right*

Medieval Revivals

...the gothic style should be recommended as being the most expressive of the Christian's hope. Pagan forms and devices, at their best, are ill adapted for a Christian burial ground.
—Wilson McCandles, *Allegheny Cemetery*, 1873

Clockwise from upper left:
Sturdy Romanesque mausoleums, resembling a row of townhouses, embody the families' desire to endure; 1890s, Graceland Cemetery, Chicago, Illinois.

Tomb combining stylistic modernity with powerful Romanesque forms; Graceland Cemetery, Chicago, Illinois.

Alone on a raised lot, the Gothic mausoleum of J.B. Ford (founder of Pittsburgh Plate Glass Company) is one of the most elaborate in America; Allegheny Cemetery, Pittsburgh, Pennsylvania.

Romanesque Schofield mausoleum; pink and grey columns and bronze doors create an unusually warm appearance; Lake View Cemetery, Cleveland, Ohio.

Clockwise from left:
1864, Mount Auburn Cemetery, Cambridge, Massachusetts.

Mid-nineteenth-century print by J. Smillie of Charlotte Canda's grave, one of the glories of Brooklyn's Green-Wood Cemetery. Today this fantastic monument, built at a cost of $10,000, is damaged, eroded and crowded by more recent mausoleums.

The Fugazy mausoleum, with a bust of the family partiarch on its front, is the largest mausoleum in this southern European-style cemetery; Italian National Cemetery, Colma, California.

Funerary monuments in the picturesque Gothic style tend to be rich in visual contrasts, combining rough stone with delicate carvings and massive earthbound walls with slender rising finials. The poetic spirit of the characteristic heavenward gestures made this style appropriate for funerary images in ways in which the earlier Romanesque style, heavy and cubic, was not. Yet "cemetery Gothic" is seldom stylistically pure; classical figures and columns, for example, are freely integrated into many designs.

Gothic, with its origin in ecclesiastical works, has been seen as "the architecture of Christianity," a style whose "lofty vaults and arches are crowded with the forms of prophets and martyrs and beautiful spirits, and seem to resound with the choral hymns of angels and archangels." The "glorious Gothic" has the single disadvantage of being more expensive than buildings and monuments in the simpler Egyptian style.

Clockwise from upper left:
Small pyramidal mausoleum of William M. Gwin, first Senator from California; 1885, Mountain View Cemetery, Oakland, California.

The Schoenhofen pyramid, with a guardian sphinx and an angel in unlikely companionship; 1893, Graceland Cemetery, Chicago, Illinois.

Massive, polished black granite mausoleum, consisting of a mastaba topped by a pyramid, designed by Louis Sullivan for lumber merchant Martin Ryerson; 1887, Graceland Cemetery, Chicago, Illinois.

Egyptian Revivals

In the Pyramid immortality...is visible and palpable.

—Jean-Francois Sobry, *De l'Architecture*, 1776

...viewed as men must view the works of man, the pyramids of Egypt derive a profound interest from their antiquity. Young, compared with the works of nature, they are, of all men's works, the most ancient. They were ancient when temples and abbeys whose ruins now alone remain, were erected, and it seems as though they would endure till long after the last traces of any building now existing, or likely to be built by modern men, has disappeared from the surface of the earth.

—Richard A. Proctor, "The Pyramid of Cheops," *The North American Review*, 1883

Unlike the classical and medieval styles, which informed buildings of nearly every type, the Egyptian Revival found expression primarily in funerary and memorial contexts. In the 1820s the New England sculptor Horatio Greenough called the obelisk "the most purely *monumental* form of structure," and he advised the Bunker Hill memorial planners to choose such an object to mark the Revolutionary War battlefield. The 555-foot tall Washington Monument, much larger in scale, was begun in 1833 to honor the father of American independence, and in 1881, Cleopatra's Needle, an Egyptian obelisk carved around 1600 B.C., was installed in Central Park in New York City. These monuments were widely visited and were publicized in magazines and books across the country. Clusters of obelisks in many cemeteries testify to the growing

popularity of the form in the second half of the nineteenth century. At Laurel Hill in Philadelphia dozens of them point to the sky and link the graves to the heavens.

Egyptian-style obelisks, columns, guardian sphinxes, and winged globes were particularly popular in the design of monuments, entrance gates and stained-glass windows of non-denominational cemeteries. Dr. Jacob Bigelow, one of the founders of Mount Auburn Cemetery, chose a sphinx to commemorate the Union dead. Pyramids, mastabas (Egyptian funerary monuments in the form of truncated pyramids) and Egyptian temples grace the graves of American statesmen and merchants. Yet some nineteenth-century observers expressed definite uneasiness about the style. An anonymous article that appeared in the *The North American Review* in 1836 states: "It is the architecture of embalmed cats and deified crocodiles: solid, stupendous, and time-defying, we allow; but associated in our minds with all that is disgusting and absurd in superstition." In order to compensate for the pagan origin of the Egyptian style, biblical citations as well as crosses and images of angels are often placed on mausoleum doors.

In rows, left to right:

Masonic memorial; Kensico Cemetery, Valhalla, New York.

The Winter mausoleum, with bronze double doors and two guardian sphinxes, is the largest private mausoleum in Allegheny Cemetery, although it contains only four crypts; Pittsburgh, Pennsylvania.

Obelisks and tall shafts soar as if to touch the sky; Laurel Hill Cemetery, Philadelphia, Pennsylvania.

Mausoleum in the form of an Egyptian temple, guarded by two sphinxes; Dodge Mausoleum, circa 1920s, Woodlawn Cemetery, Detroit, Michigan.

Sixty-five-foot obelisk on the grave of John D. Rockefeller, the largest in any American cemetery; 1899, Lake View Cemetery, Cleveland, Ohio.

Old World Images of Death

Clockwise from upper right: Reclining woman pierced by Death as she recommends her soul to God; putti with inverted torches mourn at her side; 1807, Santa Maria Novella, Florence.

Capuchin Cemetery, Church of Santa Maria de la Concezione, Rome. The profusion of human bones decorating this popular eighteenth-century cellar chapel reveals a vastly different strain of sentiment from the desire of modern cemeteries to hide all signs of bodily decay.

Relief in the chapel of Sainte Clotilde showing a recumbent man eaten by worms; in the upper section the man is shown alive again in paradise; 1468, Cathedral of Notre Dame, Paris.

It is not an unusual thing to see a marble of Death, impersonated by a grim skeleton, seizing with brutally-depicted strength the figure of the person who lies underneath the diabolical monument.

—William Crawford Hirsch,
"Monumental Art in Italian Cemeteries,"
Park and Cemetery, 1902

Why should we thus seek to clothe death with unnecessary terrors....The grave should be surrounded by everything that may inspire tenderness and veneration for the dead, or that may win the living to virtue.

—Washington Irving, *Sketchbook*, 1820

From the thirteenth through the seventeenth century, corpses and skeletons—graphic depictions of the body's fate—appeared frequently in art and literature, in images ranging from the macabre to the consoling. For instance, in many late medieval depictions of death, a rotting corpse lies in the lower part of the composition while, above, a figure representing the soul of the deceased rises into the company of God and angels. A sixteenth-century alabaster statue of a desiccated corpse once presided over the Cemetery of the Holy Innocents in Paris, the largest European burial place until modern times. And on the dramatic baroque tomb of Alexander the VII by Bernini in Saint Peter's in the Vatican, a statue of the deceased prays above the figure of a skeleton holding an hour glass, its menacing presence offset by personifications of virtues, the sacred context of the side chapel, the obvious artistry of presentation, and the hopeful message of spiritual salvation and earthly commemoration.

Living death depicted as an animated skeleton; lower part of the tomb of Giovanni Battista Gisleni, 1672, Church of Santa Maria del Popolo, Rome. *Left*

Colonial marker on the grave of Sarah Spining; 1730, Saint John Episcopal Church, Elizabeth, New Jersey. *Right*

The skulls and crossbones that form a large part of the imagery of seventeenth- and eighteenth-century Puritan graveyards offer less consolation than the artistic images of baroque Rome. When carving grave markers, local artists in the Northeast simplified European depictions of death and omitted the usual accompanying scene or symbol of the soul in reunion with God. The grim tombstones of the Puritans remain the best known representations produced by a culture that distrusted images and encouraged its members to fear death and its aftermath.

With the spread of AIDS and drug addiction, the skull has again become a major cultural symbol. Visible in hospitals, schools, housing projects, subways, and on television, skulls are a familiar presence in contemporary America.

Today's pervasive image of death is not represented in the cemetery but in the hospital. The older vision of skeletons and worms has been replaced by an emaciated person lying in bed in a strange, sanitized room. The picture is of "technological death," to use the phrase of Philippe Aries: a terminally-ill patient hooked up to life-support systems, colored plastic tubes bringing fluids to veins, electrical impulses jumping across a screen, and beeps sounding faintly. In such a setting, death usually comes in the early morning to a patient lying alone.

American Images of Death

Clockwise from upper left: Giovanni Dagostino and his son, Orazio, lie together in death; 1918, Mount Carmel Cemetery, Hillside, Illinois.

On the tomb of a Mason, this sculpted allegory of death includes Father Time, a winged hour glass, a broken column, and a female figure with a funerary urn; Lutheran Cemetery, Queens, New York.

Reclining figure of a discalced Carmelite on a deathbed strewn with roses; New Calvary Cemetery, Los Angeles, California.

It is from the very brink of the grave, where rest in eternal sleep the mortal remains of those whom we have best loved, that Christianity speaks to us in its most triumphant, soul-exalting words, of victory over death, and a life to come. Surely, then, all that man places over the tomb should, in a measure, speak the same language.

—"American Architecture," *The North American Review*, 1836

I think it is kind of atrocious. A lot of people call it the statue of death. Of course, we all know we are going to die. I don't know why you want to have that. It has been there for years.

—Cemetery administrator, on *The Grim Reaper*, Bohemian National Cemetery, Chicago, 1988

The overwhelming emphasis in American cemeteries is on hopeful images which exclude death and decay. A few jarring depictions of death have found a place in our cemeteries, and in their exceptionality, they exert an intense attraction. Texts or conversations about cemeteries tend to single out these unique images for discussion.

The Grim Reaper by Albin Polasek in Chicago's Bohemian National Cemetery is a life-sized bronze of a hooded old woman bent over a walking stick. The power of this traditional yet mysterious figure comes from her hidden face, her determined movements and her physical strength combined with her old age. *The Grim Reaper* makes the same point as her predecessors in European art: death can come in any form, anywhere and any time.

Smaller in scale, yet no less poignant as reminders of death, are the paired photographs on the Dagostino tomb depicting the corpses of thirty-two year-old Giovanni and his two year-old son, Orazio. A cemetery in Pittsburgh contains a granite monument in the form of a dead tree, standing straight and tall but truncated. Every branch is chopped off, and on the smooth surface of the cuts, the names of those who have passed away have been

recorded. There is no place for new branches on this somber memorial of 1865.

Henry Adams commissioned the famous statue popularly known as *Grief* from Augustus St. Gaudens in memory of his wife Marian, who had committed suicide. Completed in 1892, the sculpture, in Washington D.C.'s Rock Creek Cemetery, depicts a hooded bronze figure seated before a flesh-colored marble slab. The monument is on elevated ground, surrounded by a hedge of holly. The narrow stepped entrance is located behind the statue, so that one sees the figure only after having ascended into its ring-like space. A semicircular bench opposite the monument invites the visitor to contemplation. The face of the statue is cold and expressionless, the eyes half-closed. Adams stated in his autobiography that the interest of the figure lay "not in its meaning, but in the response of the observer"; people saw, he claimed, only what they brought to it. For some, the imagery of the Adams memorial may recall lines from Tennyson's *In Memoriam* (1833):

There sat the Shadow fear'd of man,
Who broke our fair companionship,
And spread his mantle dark and cold
And wrapt thee formless in the fold,
and dull'd the murmur of thy lips,...
...The Shadow sits and waits for me.

Clockwise from left:
The Grim Reaper by Albin Polasek; Stejskal Buchal Mausoleum, 1920s, Bohemian National Cemetery, Chicago, Illinois.

Adams memorial by Augustus St. Gaudens. No dates, names or explanation accompany this isolated statue; 1892, Rock Creek Cemetery, Washington, D.C.

Statue of *Death*, originally entitled "Eternal Silence," by Lorado Taft. This memorial of 1909 for the pioneer Dexter family is the most visited statue at Chicago's Graceland Cemetery; Illinois.

On a mausoleum door, a powerful bronze image of a shrouded warrior, his eyes closed in death, clasps an over-sized sword. The figure, although upright, recalls portraits of recumbent knights carved on medieval tombs; Woodlawn Cemetery, the Bronx, New York.

Images of Grief

A woman covers her eyes while carrying a funerary urn; 1847, Mount Auburn Cemetery, Cambridge, Massachusetts. *Top left*

Classical relief of a woman in a conventional mourning pose; Mount Auburn Cemetery, Cambridge, Massachusetts. *Bottom left*

The effects of grief: weighed down by sorrow, uplifted by hope; Rich Memorial, 1879, Mount Auburn Cemetery, Cambridge, Massachusetts. - *Center*

This personification of mourning is unusual because of the powerful physicality of the female form; 1930s, Woodlawn Cemetery, the Bronx, New York. *Right*

Thou has come home bearing rare sheaves of courage, faith, love and patience.

—Rebecca, Mount Auburn Cemetery, Cambridge

Nearly all the statues are of women, angels or children.

—Henry P. Phelps, *The Albany Rural Cemetery*, 1893

The grieving figure of a young woman, her head inclined, her eyes closed, constitutes the most popular visual symbol of perpetual sorrow. Mourning female figures grace the grave stelae of classical Greece. Christian art provides similar images of Mary Magdalene—sorrowfully embracing the crucifix or visiting Jesus's tomb in the company of two other women. Other monuments represent the Pietà—the Virgin Mary lamenting over her dead son, or Mary alone, her head covered with a hood, praying for the dead. The noble artistic origin of the mourning figure virtually assured its revival.

As early as 1839, Moses King, author of a guidebook to Mount Auburn Cemetery, noted that "weeping female figures" had been placed on several family tombs. For more than a century thereafter, images of grieving women in classical robes, often leaning against a column, carrying an urn with the remains of the deceased or bearing a wreath as a tribute, proliferated in burial places throughout the country. Judging from the names on the tombs, this feminine imagery of grief was deemed equally appropriate for the graves of women and men.

Depictions of grief can encompass various other emotions, such as resignation and hope. Female figures, turning their gaze forever heavenward, sometimes connote intercession on behalf of the dead or perhaps silent communication with those who have departed. Other such figures, however, are stark, impenetrable presences conveying a sense of the immense gap between life and death.

Aestheticized grief; mausoleum window depicting a mourning woman, her head resting on a column topped by an urn; Woodlawn Cemetery, the Bronx, New York. *Left*

Lamenting female figure in bronze recalls the Virgin Mary at the Crucifixion; Bohemian National Cemetery, Chicago, Illinois. *Center*

The weight of grief is visualized in this graceful sculpture of a woman in classical garb; 1861, Oak Hill Cemetery, Washington, D.C. *Right*

Images of Voluptuousness

Clockwise from upper left:
The tomb of the late Secretary of State John Hay; 1905, Lake View Cemetery, Cleveland, Ohio.

Oak Woods Cemetery, Chicago, Illinois.

1918, Nisky Hills Cemetery, Bethlehem Pennsylvania.

Reproduction of Italian Antonio Canova's *Cupid and Psyche*, available when one buys eight burial places; Hollywood Memorial Cemetery, Los Angeles, California, 1988.

Mori memorial by Raymond Hood; 1931, Woodlawn Cemetery, the Bronx, New York.

The soul being released; Warner family tomb by Alexander Milne Calder; Laurel Hill Cemetery, Philadelphia, Pennsylvania.

One man dies, another too, hundreds of others all became conceived in the intensity of love.

—Corrado Maltese, *Staglieno*, 1974

In elite cemeteries, life-sized, sensuously portrayed figures of shapely young women are a common but arresting sight. The motif takes the form of a bashful yet explicitly sexual young maiden; classical robes and a gesture toward heaven—the new domicile of the deceased—provide a veneer of decorous conventionality to these images of voluptuousness.

On a bronze mausoleum door, sculpted women press themselves against the grating, their transparent veils draped to reveal youthful bodies, sleek and slender, as they seek to enter the chilled house of the dead. One figure inscribes the words "Yet Shall He Live" on a tall granite shaft; the torsion in her pose against the flat face of the monument highlights her fullness.

Reference to male sexuality is rare, made mainly by the occasional shaft exhibiting a strong phallic form. In Bethlehem, Pennsylvania, for example, an assertive monument of that type evoked so much embarrassment and curiosity that a local clergyman asked the cemetery administrator if he could "do anything to remove that monument." Located near the entrance to Nisky Hills Cemetery, the memorial was delivered by horse and buggy in 1918. The current administrator, who refers to the shaft as "the bullet," explains that in 1918 the cemetery had no regulations concerning "what was to be erected on the lot" and thus "no idea of what was coming in." "The bullet," he says, "changed everything; after that you had to submit a description and a drawing before you could erect a monument."

Clockwise from left:

Female inscribing the Smith Memorial "yet shall he live"; Riverside Cemetery, Waterbury, Connecticut.

Luyties Memorial, known as "the girl in the shadow box"; early 1900s, Bellefontaine Cemetery, St. Louis, Missouri.

Strikingly animated female figure recalling the nymphs of classical myths; 1932, Woodlawn Cemetery, the Bronx, New York.

On this bronze mausoleum door, grief is expressed by tender young nudes, whose fashionably slender proportions update their Grecian reference; Woodlawn Cemetery, the Bronx, New York.

Portrait of Oscar Spindler, his profile turned towards a young, life-sized woman; 1894, Oak Woods Cemetery, Chicago, Illinois.

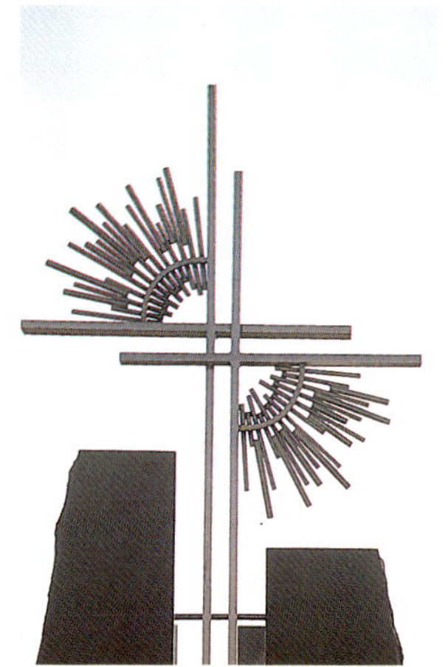

Crosses

Clockwise from upper left:
Slavic cross; 1972, Lake View Cemetery, Seattle, Washington.

Nameless wooden cross in a small cemetery near Trenton, New Jersey.

Modernist stainless steel cross; 1970s, St. Casimir Lithuanian Cemetery, Chicago, Illinois.

Rusty cross of pipes; Woodland Cemetery, Newark, New Jersey.

Sculpted ivy-covered tree in the form of a cross; 1882, Calvary Cemetery, Queens, New York.

Cross made from birch logs; St. Nicholas Ukranian Cemetery, Chicago, Illinois.

Simple stone cross; The Evergreens Cemetery, Brooklyn, New York.

Around and within view from that hill-top [in Green-Wood Cemetery, Brooklyn] were probably more than a thousand various memorial stones, and among them all I counted but four crosses.

—Halford L. Mills, "American Cemeteries are Pagan," *Park and Cemetery*, 1895

We bow before thy cross, oh master, and we glorify thy holy Resurrection.

—Epitaph, Washelli Cemetery, Seattle, 1971

The seventeenth-century Puritan settlers of the New World detested the cross, seeing it as a symbol of Roman Catholicism. Indeed, their counterparts in England went so far as to propose changing the names of Red Cross Street, White Cross Street and Charing Cross to words less objectionable. They argued "that thus all profaneness being rooted out and extirpated from our conventions nothing but holiness may remain among us." In Rhode Island, Roger Williams called the cross a "badge of superstition," and in Massachusetts in 1634, John Endicott publicly cut out the cross from the English flag with his sword. Thus, the absence of crosses from New England church yards comes as no surprise. Not until the 1870s, with the popular revival of Gothic architecture, did many Protestants begin to accept the cross as a general emblem

of Christian hope. In Catholic cemeteries, by contrast, crosses have always been common and prominently displayed. According to Father Kezys, a Chicago Jesuit, "If there is no cross, something essential is missing: a symbol of being Christian."

The most common symbol of Christianity has long been present in cemeteries of the Southwest, where individually designed, handmade wooden crosses are still popular with Mexican-Americans. Unfortunately, when exposed to the hot sunlight of the region, these simple, often beautiful markers dry out and crumble; cemetery caretakers periodically collect and burn the fragments.

By 1989, because most cemeteries prohibited upright markers, new crosses were rarely seen in isolation. Indeed, of the more than two hundred markers illustrated in the trade brochures of monument dealers, only one was a freestanding cross. Unassertive small crosses, carved in relief, however, formed part of the ornamentation on over half the markers.

Cross with a photograph of a seventeen year-old Italian immigrant; 1917, Italian National Cemetery, Colma, California. *Left*

Image of the sorrowful Christ on a stone cross; 1940s, St. Casimir Lithuanian Cemetery, Chicago, Illinois. *Center*

Heavy homemade iron cross supporting a tiny Christ marks a nameless grave near the former steel town of Roebling, New Jersey. *Top right*

Christ on the cross; St. Casimir Lithuanian Cemetery, Chicago, Illinois. *Bottom right*

Resurrection Angels

Metal marker depicting an angel who pulls a boat carrying the deceased; in front burns the torch of life; 1903, Lake View Cemetery, Seattle, Washington. *Top left*

Unusually refined image of an angel on Christ's tomb; Elkins family mausoleum, circa 1900, Laurel Hill Cemetery, Philadelphia, Pennsylvania. *Bottom left*

Two angels in flight look heavenward across a river; The Evergreens Cemetery, Brooklyn, New York. *Top center*

Woodlawn Cemetery, the Bronx, New York. *Bottom center*

Angel blowing a trumpet to raise the dead; 1906, Woodlawn Cemetery, the Bronx, New York. *Right*

Angelic forms...have been favorite subjects of monumental sculpture. It could hardly be otherwise. Our earliest and most cherished associations have accustomed us to blend some image of cherub or seraph, with every thought of the spiritual world. Sacred verse, from the nursery rhyme to the lofty epic, has made these winged messengers of heaven seem almost familiar to our senses.

—Nehemiah Cleaveland, *Green-Wood Illustrated*, 1847

Among images meant to dispel or soften the finality of death, angels are the most common. Although visible in a variety of forms, they all represent messengers from heaven who remind the living of the gospel's good news. "He has risen. He is not there," is a familiar inscription beneath the angel who points to the sky, telling of Christ's resurrection. "Mama the angels will meet me soon," proclaims the epitaph of seven year-old Albertina Coles, buried at Woodlawn Cemetery in the Bronx in 1892. A stained-glass window in Lutheran Cemetery in Queens shows angels with powerful wings carrying the deceased "Towards a Better World." In a metal relief, the angel propels the ship of the dead.

During the eighties, symbols of immortality were more muted than in previous decades. Angels, in their rare appearance on these contemporary monuments, tend to be small, praying figures traced onto markers, rather than free-standing figures. Relegated to the role of substitute mourner, the angel has lost its function as the messenger of hope or as the celestial guide and companion to heaven.

Clockwise from left:

A large bronze statue of a resurrection angel forms the centerpiece of a monument designed to suggest the gate of heaven; 1905, The Evergreens Cemetery, Brooklyn, New York.

Angel sitting on Christ's open sepulchre indicates to the three Marys that Christ has risen; St. Michael's Cemetery, Queens, New York.

Christian soul in the form of an angel wearing white robes; from above, a star showers light; 1920s, Woodlawn Cemetery, the Bronx, New York.

Angel within a cathedral of trees; 1912, Moravian Cemetery, Staten Island, New York.

At the heart of Newark's Central Ward a blond angel adorns the window of a lavish mausoleum from the 1920s; Fairmount Cemetery, Newark, New Jersey.

Landscapes

Sunset, meandering stream, an autumn tree; 1928, Woodlawn Cemetery, the Bronx, New York. *Left*

Open tulips and a sinking red sun reflected in water; 1930, Kensico Cemetery, Valhalla, New York. *Right*

Eye has not seen, nor ear heard, neither have entered into the hearts of man, the things that God has prepared for him / Corinthians 1

—Epitaph, Woodlawn Cemetery, the Bronx, 1966

Within the landscape of the cemetery are other landscapes, outlined in stone or rendered in color on mausoleum windows. Portraits of the house of the deceased, landscapes of recreation, quiet scenes of natural beauty, even when rugged or tinged with autumn colors, all suggest paradise both on earth and beyond the grave.

In epitaphs, paradise is a place away from the noise and confusion of life where "there is peace," and God is present. "Thine eyes shall see the king in his beauty," on that "shore where they weep and suffer and fear no more." Those dead are forever united with their families and friends: "Parting and sorrow they shall know no more."

In the first three decades of the twentieth century, landscapes were very popular in the colored glass of mausoleum windows, just as they were in churches and the homes of the rich. But the landscapes in mausoleums, although lovely, tend to have a feeling of remoteness; rarely are they populated by human figures. Instead, flowing from the mountains or hills in the far distance is the meandering "river of life." The sun is low on the horizon, and the water reflects the color of the sky. Flowers blossom, and evergreens, especially cypresses and yews, grow on the banks of the water. All of these natural forms take on symbolic meaning given their funereal context.

There are only a few cemetery images that exude an otherworldliness which transcends everyday life. One of them is the window to the Matthews mausoleum, a hand-tinted photograph of a boating party on a tree shaded winding river. There is a haunting quality to the scene's quiet stillness, the formality of the grouping and the ghostly appearance of its fading figures.

Clockwise from left:

Landscape of life: river, evergreens, lilies, and the setting sun; Mount Pleasant Cemetery, Newark, New Jersey.

Melancholic autumn landscape under a cloudy sky; 1926, The Evergreens Cemetery, Brooklyn, New York.

In this companion to the adjacent image, a meandering river cuts through snowy hills; The Evergreens Cemetery, Brooklyn, New York.

Image of "Psalm 1" recalls the man who is "like a tree planted near running water, that yields its fruit in due season and whose leaves never fade" and who delights in the Lord's law; 1928, Graceland Cemetery, Chicago, Illinois.

Matthews mausoleum, circa 1920, Nisky Hills Cemetery, Bethlehem, Pennsylvania.

1944, Kensico Cemetery, Valhalla, New York.

THE CONTEMPORARY CEMETERY

In the last decade of the twentieth century, American cemeteries seem anachronistic and irrelevant. To many, they occupy valuable space which could be put to better use. To others, they are almost invisible. They are unvisited, unloved and unimportant. A century ago, cemeteries stood, along with hospitals, churches and schools, as major institutions of urban life. By 1989, with the rise of cremation, they were rarely even primary places of remembrance.

The Cemetery as a Business

Clockwise from upper left:
Billboard showing attractive older couple exchanging loving looks while resting in the late afternoon sun of Forest Lawn; Glendale Avenue, Glendale, California, 1984.

Large monument shaped like a billboard commemorates the McCarthy family; 1964, Lindenwood Cemetery, Fort Wayne, Indiana.

Flat marble front of modern community mausoleum; the names of the dead are inscribed on its smooth surface; Rosedale Cemetery, Linden, New Jersey, 1981.

Homogenous markers cover a Jewish section of Oak Ridge Cemetery; Hillside, Illinois, 1986.

From the original idea of our brother Charles Nichols was devised the scheme of meeting at a given place once a year for the exchange of experiences and to visit the various cemeteries.

—George W. Creesy, President, Association of American Cemetery Superintendents, Tenth Annual Convention, Cincinnati, 1897

I am more and more convinced that the greatest practical good resulting from our meeting will be the general increase of knowledge in regard to how cemeteries can be made beautiful.

—O.C. Simmonds, Association of American Cemetery Superintendents, Annual Convention, Omaha, 1898

In 1987, the American Cemetery Association celebrated its centennial. In its early days as the American Association of Cemetery Superintendents, it was an articulate group with a distinctive middle-American leadership. Its most prominent members tended to be administrators of elite rural cemeteries, men such as O.C. Simonds of Graceland (Chicago), Carl E. Kern of Spring Grove (Cincinnati), Frank Eurich of Woodlawn (Toledo), and George Creesy of Harmony Grove (Salem). Their three-part motto was Unity, Growth and Knowledge—Unity because members knew that death and commemoration "would naturally cause differences of opinion"; Growth—because they wanted their group to include every major burial place in the country; and Knowledge—because they expected to teach and to learn about management, gardening, monuments, street planning, and labor relations.

Superintendents referred to themselves as "mayors of cities of the dead," responsible for the upkeep, planning, policing, financial supervision, public relations, and sometimes even the advertising of their cemeteries. Their work gave them a special opportunity to study, shape and take delight in nature.

Grave of a ten year-old girl: the headless statue of a plump girl carrying flowers in her upraised skirt conveys promises unfulfilled; 1894, Riverside Cemetery, Waterbury, Connecticut. *Left*

Thousands of modest markers in Calvary Cemetery reflect the large, Catholic, blue-collar population of Waterbury, Connecticut, 1982. *Right*

Park and Cemetery, the association's monthly magazine, discussed ways to implement a landscape vision based on poetry, painting and gardening. The journal included approving references to the theories of J.C. Loudon, John Ruskin, A.J. Downing, and F.L. Olmsted. But it gave the greatest weight to the ideas of Adolf Strauch, the innovative superintendent of Cincinnati's Spring Grove Cemetery. Strauch was deemed "the most artistic in his taste and the most progressive in his ideas of what a cemetery should be, of any man that has lived in this country." He assigned preeminence to nature, not monuments, a concept that greatly influenced the design of rural cemeteries.

Cemetery superintendents were distressed that the general public showed little appreciation for their contribution to the beautification of cities. It was a bittersweet occasion for superintendents when visitors streamed in on Memorial Day and All Saint's Day; proud to show off their cemeteries to such large crowds, at the same time officials were fearful of the damage that people might cause to their carefully arranged landscapes.

It was not until the 1950s that a dramatic loss of interest in the cemetery as a place of commemoration allowed administrators to dictate the use of their grounds. Cemeteries, however, had come to be managed by salesmen who thought more about increasing revenues than about beautifying the landscape. The American Cemetery Association neglected its goal of creating and maintaining beautiful landscapes: instead "God's Acre" became an aggressive business. While individuals with a poetic vision had once reigned, by the 1980s, the large-scale conglomerates of funeral homes, cemeteries and related industries dictated a commercial view that successfully applied the chain-store model. Robert L. Waltrip, the founder and chairman of Service Corporation International expressed his vision to turn the corporation into "the True Value hardware of the funeral-service industry." By 1989, his company was handling a full five percent of the nation's funerals and reporting $540 million in annual revenues. Perhaps more importantly, it owned 13,000 acres of real estate. While Joseph Hillhouse, Jacob Bigelow, Adolph Strauch, and Hubert Eaton changed the style, outlook and philosophy of the cemetery, the vision offered by the young corporations is limited to making a profit.

Neglected Cemeteries

Boarded-up mausoleum surrounded by fallen fragments; Waldheim Cemetery, Forest Park, Illinois, 1983. *Left*

Overgrown Chinese-American "Celestial Hill" section of The Evergreens Cemetery features small crooked markers peeping up through the tall grass; Brooklyn, New York. *Right*

The Board of Directors of Oak Hill Cemetery Association has voted to abandon 118-year-old Oak Hill Cemetery [Atchinson, Kansas], and was expected to file dissolution papers. The Board is said to have about $90 in its bank account. The cemetery, still active, has been averaging 32 burials a year.

—"Cemetery News Notes," *American Cemetery*, July 1982

Aesthetically, an overgrown cemetery is as much a liability to a neighborhood as vacant land collecting debris and propagating weeds.

—*Cemeteries as Open Space Reservations*, HUD Report, 1970

Whenever a cemetery runs out of land for burial, its revenues diminish drastically. At the same time, expenses continue: money is needed for lawn care and new plantings as well as for trained personnel to discourage thieves and vandals and to restore toppled markers. If the cemetery does not have a perpetual care fund, its income dries up, and it cannot maintain its grounds. Unused cemeteries, left unguarded, often become garbage dumps or places where local teenagers have parties, race motorcycles and vent their boredom and frustration by toppling monuments. As a fourteen year-old boy who had damaged seventy-three monuments in Morristown, New Jersey explained, "it [is] something to do."

Muggers benefitting from the isolation of the grounds prey easily upon elderly people who continue to visit the cemetery. Vandals rob cars and snatch purses from mourners. Others prefer to steal from the dead and go so far as to open coffins, ghoulishly searching for gold fillings and valuables.

Local organizations such as the Boy Scouts, the Fire Department or a church may try to improve the appearance of a neglected cemetery by repairing the fences and removing the underbrush and garbage. In academic settings and elite institutions, preservationists may speak of restoring funerary monuments that have historical or artistic value, and the more ambitious among them might like to restore entire cemeteries. But without continual attention, these efforts do not last long, and within a few years the burial ground regains its derelict look.

A few well-known cemeteries continue to attract the general public. They organize photography contests that use the monuments and the grounds as subject matter and conduct gardening classes that include practical demonstrations of tree pruning and flower planting. Forest Lawn in Glendale is famous for weddings celebrated at the cemetery chapels, and Cedar Lawn in Chicago keeps deer, peacocks and a horse named "Elegant Sam." But most cemeteries do not actively encourage visitors.

Clockwise from upper left:
The Dorchester Burial Ground, more than three centuries old and the resting place of two colonial governors and other prominent people, is badly maintained and closed to the public; Dorchester, Massachusetts, 1984.

Like an open meadow of variegated grasses, its tombstones almost invisible, Woodland Cemetery has become a place of beauty after years of neglect; Newark, New Jersey, 1988.

Wreckage of once orderly rows of tombstones; St. Michael's Cemetery, Queens, New York, 1983.

In this "German-Romantic" landscape, heavy monuments, now broken, crooked or toppled, mark overgrown plots; at the center, as if on stage, kneels the lamenting Magdalene, dramatically grasping the cross; circa 1890s, St. Michael's Cemetery, Queens, New York.

Eroded Monuments

In rows, left to right:
The nearly obliterated portrait of a young Russian man; 1911, Lake View Cemetery, Seattle, Washington.

A sculpture of two children fades into abstraction; Saint Mary's Cemetery, Cincinnati, Ohio.

The spectral, dissolved face of a child; circa 1870s, Graceland Cemetery, Chicago, Illinois.

A portrait from a family mausoleum retains some of its original grand formality and realism in spite of the wearing away of the paint surface; 1907, Woodlawn Cemetery, the Bronx, New York.

This Virgin Mary, after a century of erosion, has become a figure of death; Holy Cross Cemetery, Brooklyn, New York.

We are subject to the extremes of heat and cold, of moisture and dryness; to intense frosts and sudden thaws. No material that can be used for monuments has yet to be found perfectly proof against these potent influences.

—Nehemiah Cleaveland, *Green-Wood Illustrated*, 1847

Although marble monuments typically were sold with the promise of permanence, in less than a century, most have become badly eroded, their inscriptions unreadable. Rates of deterioration vary according to location, with urban tombstones sometimes decaying ten times as rapidly as those in rural graveyards. According to geographer Thomas C. Meierding, the most serious airborne pollutant is gaseous sulfer dioxide, which spurs the growth of the gypsum crystals that cause marble to shed large flakes and lose strength.

Marble breaks down as a result of pollution and extreme temperature changes. Delicate carvings lose the lines that describe a face; shapes become distorted; the organic forms of figures are reduced to abstract geometric

volumes. Photographs and colored glass windows fade, leaving blurred outlines and fragmented portraits. Most cemeteries do not accept responsibility for such deterioration. The family is only asked to repair a monument if its unstable condition poses a safety hazard. Often a damaged monument is simply removed.

In 1989, more durable materials, granite and bronze, were those most commonly used for funerary monuments. Granite is said to erode only one eighth of an inch every one hundred thousand years. But although granite can withstand the ravages of time, it is very expensive to carve or inscribe, and it lacks marble's capacity to represent life-like forms and warm surface effects, both important in rendering the human figure.

Erosion adds a new feeling of grace and spirituality to this sculpture of an angel; Mount Pleasant Cemetery, Newark, New Jersey. *Left*

Red granite marker commemorates monument maker Anton Bohm and his wife. A *tour de force* of Bohm's craft, the monument was designed to last for centuries; the long text is written in exquisite Gothic letters, which, like the crest with the tools of the deceased's trade, are unerringly carved deep into the stone; 1963, Crown Hill Cemetery, Denver, Colorado. *Right*

Highgate Cemetery, London

Clockwise from upper left:
Egyptian Avenue, Highgate Cemetery; this ivy-covered burial ground became a popular setting for horror movies.

Only a cross and a statue are visible in this overgrown section of Highgate, an unexpected wilderness near the center of the city.

As the British lion sleeps, ivy, a symbol of remembrance, creates anonymity by covering markers in green; Highgate Cemetery.

Tall monuments rising behind a screen of trees and bushes in the semi-abandoned Victorian cemetery of Abney Park, London.

The roof of its shelter fallen, an intimate sculptural group is now exposed to the elements; Kensal Green Cemetery, London.

Statues were vandalized and occultism, voodoo and witchcraft began to flourish. The setting, unfortunately, was all too perfect. It is not difficult to imagine these graves yawning at midnight and vampires returning before the first rays of sun.

—Felix Barker, *Highgate Cemetery*, 1984

London's fashionable Highgate Cemetery was established on thirty-six acres in the southwest sector of the city in 1837. For well over a century, the cemetery provided the final resting place for many of the rich and famous of the British empire, and it ranked among the dozen most famous necropolises on earth. Highgate is small in comparison to the cemeteries of the United States, yet it provides an important example; after four decades of almost complete neglect, nature has taken over the grounds and covered the monuments. Plant life—sycamores, ivy and ferns—smother, crack and topple the monuments.

In 1975, after 138 years of existence, Highgate went bankrupt. Six years later, it was bought for fifty pounds by a non-profit corporation devoted to the upkeep of this historic place, The Friends of Highgate Cemetery. In a

Amidst the general neglect of Highgate Cemetery one encounters arresting statues as well as some of the most outstanding roses in London. *Left*

The only family plot to have survived the surrounding destruction is that of Karl Marx, the prophet of the demise of capitalism. While the tombs of Marx's neighbors suffered from both nature and vandals, his remains and those of his family were moved to a large plot in the new section of Highgate. Dominated by a fierce-looking granite bust of the old revolutionary, the Marx family grave is the most visited in London. The epitaph, in gold letters, reads, "Workers of All Lands Unite"; 1963. *Right*

nation long fascinated by the poetic possibilities of ruins, Highgate was bound to find supporters. Today there is no question of restoring Highgate to its tidy pre-World War II look. The task that the present owners have set for themselves is to preserve the ruined cemetery in the manner that best displays its mystery and Victorian gloom. To do this, the administration must open up paths, remove the layer of green from the "most interesting monuments," cut the threatening trees, control the roosting pigeons, and stop vandalism; no small task, but more manageable than maintaining the cemetery as it was during its heyday.

The fate of Highgate Cemetery is not unique. Other fashionable London cemeteries, such as Abney Park and Kensal Green, have suffered similar neglect. Both elite and ordinary urban cemeteries in the United States may one day come to the same fate. Laurel Hill Cemetery in Philadelphia, now in dire financial straits, could be the first of a series of American necropolises to be reduced to magnificent ruins. Thorny bushes would make it difficult to move through the grounds, yet those adventurous enough to proceed would see surprising views: ivy connecting the tall crooked obelisks like threads in a spider web and broken granite mausolea covered with plants and moss—scenes of nature's dominance accompanied by the chirping of birds.

Alternative Uses of Cemeteries

Life-sized statue of Robert L. Kellner; this likeness of Kellner, who was killed in the forest of Argonne, France in 1918, coincidentally adorns a forest-like section of run-down St. Michael's Cemetery; Queens, New York. *Top*

In the old Camden Cemetery, the condition of the semi-abandoned burial place is similar to that of the nearby houses; the city plans to relocate the markers and the remains to the New Camden Cemetery; Camden, New Jersey, 1982. *Left*

This old cemetery, situated in a residential neighborhood of Bridgeport, Connecticut, has become a soccer field for local children; 1982. *Right*

Because of land depletion for building sites, legislation was enacted in 1921 and 1923 to remove all cemeteries from the city [San Francisco] and to prohibit further burials. Most graves were moved from the four cemeteries to a small town located south of San Francisco. Colma (formerly Lawndale) became "Cemetery City" with the development of new burial acreage after the relocation of over 90,000 remains from the outlawed cemeteries.

—*Cemeteries as Open Space Reservations*, HUD report, 1970

One of the most sacred and enduring human ties is that by which the hearts of men are bounded to the burial places of their departed friends, and no residence can be permanently regarded as HOME which is not also identified prospective or actually, with the memory of those we love.

—D.B. Douglass, President, Board of Trustees, Green-Wood Cemetery, Brooklyn, 1839

Even though the United States is a vast, underpopulated continental nation, the two million acres occupied by cemeteries tend to be strategically located and economically valuable. As an administrator at Seattle's Lake View Cemetery, which overlooks Puget Sound, remarked: "This is the most valuable real estate in the city. There are a lot of developers who would give an arm and a leg to build condos here." More and more, a process of cemetery land conversion is taking place. In one successful assault by urban improvement on the cemetery, Old Harmony Cemetery in northeast Washington, D.C. disappeared after its twenty-nine acres of land became part of a proposed highway interchange. More recently, the discovery of 900 skeletons at an ancient burial ground in Hawaii scarcely delayed the construction of an eighty million dollar beachfront hotel on Maui in 1989. Why, after all, should a few old bones stand in the way of progress?

Although private investors covet cemetery acres for obvious financial reasons, city planners and other government officials are sometimes equally contemptuous of the use of these spaces for burial. They regard graveyards as costly, useless, wasteful, and ugly, as places that take away

scarce space from the living, as fields filled with repetitive kitsch objects. Their argument is simple: Why should the dead monopolize resources that could otherwise improve their citizens' quality of life? Government agencies begin to have their eye on under-utilized or neglected cemeteries as "passive recreational space"—that is, as little used but scenic land. The city removes the broken monuments, and the grounds become an unofficial neighborhood park, with only the largest and most solidly built funerary monuments left standing.

A particularly serious threat to the cemetery is posed by the Department of Housing and Urban Development. A 1970 HUD report gave sanction to the view that burial grounds serve only a transitory and unimportant purpose. As a way to preserve the best land for needed services, the HUD report suggested that the unused space under elevated highways or in "sanitary fills" be landscaped to provide burial space. Regarding the recommendation to inter people near airports, the report suggested: "Though the problem of noise may be a disadvantage during funeral proceedings, it should be noted that the living would benefit ultimately by more separation from the noise of airports." The contrast with the nineteenth-century view of the cemetery as a place of quiet repose could not be more startling. The HUD report assumes that graves are visited only during funeral proceedings. In this conception, there is no need for an environment conducive to communion with the dead, a place hallowed by love and prayer, a place to localize one's grief—concepts so vital a century ago.

Clockwise from upper left:

Tombstones echoing the outline of Manhattan skyscrapers—the play of similar shapes raises the inevitable comparison between the world of the living and that of the dead; Calvary Cemetery, Queens, New York.

The strong grey silhouette of the Pulaski Highway borders this poor section, with simple homemade markers, of Holy Name Cemetery; Jersey City, New Jersey.

Small cluster of gravestones in the abandoned Waldheim Cemetery, Gary, Indiana. The land is to be reclaimed by the Small Farms Project of the Federal Department of Housing and Urban Development; 1983.

Small tombstones in the children's section of Nisky Hills Cemetery and the huge abandoned steel plant across the river; Bethlehem, Pennsylvania.

Visiting the Grave

In rows, left to right:
Visiting her younger brother's grave, a woman calls the adjacent plot "my bungalow"; Evergreen Cemetery, Chicago, Illinois, 1985.

Memorial Day; California, 1985.

Three generations of Vasquezes cleaning the grave of their *abuelo* (grandfather); Dade Memorial Park, Miami, Florida, 1984.

Memorial Day; Mountain View Cemetery, Fresno, California, 1985.

White metal lawn furniture welcomes visitors; 1969, Rosedale Cemetery, Linden, New Jersey.

Mrs. Sanchez asked to be buried in New York so that her children could visit her grave often; Saint Raymond's Cemetery, the Bronx, New York, 1987.

Why should they come? Coming out to the cemetery really does not do any good....Maybe some day when they are with the kids in town they visit the cemetery to show them where grandma is buried—like they would go visit an old house they once lived in.
—Cemetery administrator, Hillside, Illinois, 1986

From the time of their beginnings in the early nineteenth century, garden type cemeteries received a great deal of traffic, but the visitors came less to mourn or commemorate than to escape the crowded and noisy settings of home and work. As grounds filled with monuments and the cemetery's burial function became more explicit, urban dwellers turned to the newly created public parks.

While famous cemeteries like Arlington in Washington, D.C., Forest Lawn in Los Angeles and Saint Louis in New Orleans have always attracted tourists, and sightseers flock to the small, unnamed, picturesque cemeteries that dot the countryside, statistics about recent cemetery visitation to the average urban and rural cemetery are hard to find. Fragmentary evidence clearly indicates that cemeteries were much more heavily visited a century ago than they have been since World War II. Rochester's Mount Hope Cemetery, for example, reported in 1909 that between five and eight hundred people visited the grounds on a weekday, with the number climbing on Sundays to three to five thousand. Eight decades later, Mount Hope received less than a fifth the number of visitors. Moreover, many of these modern visitors come not to pay respect to

Clockwise from left:

Flowers and a pumpkin adorn the grave of a teenage boy; Forest Lawn Cemetery, Forest Park, Illinois, 1983.

Homemade Christmas decorations made of colorful bows and a cross adorn a grave in Saint Adalbert Cemetery, Niles, Illinois; 1984.

Located in a rarely visited, nineteenth-century Irish section of Calvary Cemetery, the recent tomb of the Evangelista family adds color with its fresh flowers and silvery birthday balloon; 1972, Queens, New York.

Teddy bear presides over a child's grave; Evergreen Cemetery, Camden, New Jersey, 1981.

the dead but to tour a site designated a landmark by the Landmarks Society of Western New York.

Today one typically views the cemetery from the outside while traveling by car. Cemetery officials are happy with this isolation and with their freedom from traffic jams, numerous mourners and excessive litter. The general public's lack of interest has given administrators a chance to impose regulations that make upkeep easier and less expensive. The process is circular. The outlawing of expressive monuments and decorations robs the cemetery of the personality and the individuality necessary for commemoration, which in turn diminishes the public's interest even further.

The regular family visit to the cemetery has become a thing of the past. An eerie feeling of isolation prevails. Even Memorial Day no longer includes the once-obligatory trip by local school children to soldiers' graves. Now people generally enter a cemetery only for the actual burial of a friend or family member. A middle-aged man from New Jersey recently explained: "When somebody dies in my family, we go out to the cemetery, but never back again. We're not the kind of people who go to the cemetery and throw flowers. Our family members are buried somewhere you are likely to be mugged, anyway."

For the most part, the elderly and a few recent immigrant groups continue to accord the cemetery an important place in their lives. Every weekend, hundreds of Hispanic visitors crowd the newer sections of Saint Raymond's Cemetery in the Bronx and as many as fifteen thousand people come on Mother's Day. At Saint Raymond's, well-tended family graves display fresh flowers, plantings and greeting cards. Families pray together in front of their markers while mourners weep without embarrassment. In contrast, members of ethnic groups who have been in America for generations and who earlier displayed their emotions openly—like the Irish and the Italians—now vent their grief at home.

The Rise of Cremation

Ancient Roman urns—richly carved with ivy, doves, rams, fruits, figures, and flowers, symbols of remembrance, peace, and life—contrast with the machine-made urns used in America today; Vatican Museum, Vatican City.

And wrap around my frame a robe of fire,
And let it rise as incense censor flung,
Until in ether pure, it may inspire
To greet the stars along the azure flung.

—"A Brief Outline of the History of the United States Cremation Corporation," circa 1933

The first crematorium in the United States was erected in 1876 in Washington, Pennsylvania. By the turn of the century, many large, non-sectarian cemeteries operated crematoriums on their grounds. Cemetery officials saw the rising popularity of cremation as a way to gain more control over the buildings and the landscape, not as a threat to the economic viability of their institutions.

However as early as 1895, a note in *Park and Cemetery* predicted that the ashes of the dead would again be placed in churches, so that: "Heaven and earth would thus seem closer together. There would be no more removals of the relics of the dead miles away out of our sight, and that devotion to the dead which at present prompts the erection of great piles of carved stone beside a grave, effecting no good purpose whatsoever, would lead to the enriching and beautifying of the House of God. . . ." Surprisingly, the magazine editors did not find this prediction of an end to cemetery burials disturbing.

Cremation, until recently opposed by some religions as a desecration of the body and an obstacle to resurrection, is now encouraged by many churches. Hundreds of congregations have developed modern equivalents of the old

Large mausoleum and columbarium; 1920s, Cypress Lawn Cemetery, Colma, California. *Top*

Paired urns shaped like books, a popular type; 1955, Rosedale Cemetery, Los Angeles, California. *Left*

1940s, Bohemian National Cemetery, Chicago, Illinois. *Right*

church graveyard in the form of memorial gardens for the scattering of ashes, thus giving new life to a powerful old concept: bringing together living and dead members of a congregation next to the "House of God."

In the United States, cremation has risen from a fraction of one percent of disposals in 1920 to more than three and one-half percent in 1961, to thirteen percent in 1986. By 1987, a third of all deaths in California, Alaska, Hawaii, Oregon, and Washington resulted in cremation, and predictions claim that by 1995 cremation will account for thirty percent of all American dispositions. As a result, cemeteries are frantically attempting to retain their function as active burial places. Leslie I. Dyer of the National Cremation Society states that "cremation is the prime topic of conversation at any place cemeterians, funeral directors or cremationists gather." "Many funeral homes will go belly-up, and many cemetery lots will go unsold," noted a trade official at a conference of cemetery salesmen in 1981. He asked an audience, "How many of you put the remains in a coffee can?" When several hands went up, he replied: "You are establishing a cheap trend," and added, "cremation must be dignified." Another speaker enlarged upon this: "Memorialization is what is selling." He predicted that niches would be made of marble and granite and perhaps be glass-fronted and that urns may cost $600 to $800.

The likelihood that cremation will continue to increase in popularity was confirmed by a 1986 survey of one hundred students at the University of California at Los Angeles, the University of Dayton and Columbia University. Nearly two-thirds of the respondents expressed the desire to be cremated at death, and the overwhelming majority wished their ashes to be scattered in some reunion with nature: "underneath an orange tree"; "spread out in the High Sierras"; "sprinkled over the start of a river to travel down to the sea"; "mixed in the sand at Santa Monica Beach." Both practices—scattering of ashes and keeping them in a container at home—obviate the need for a cemetery.

Mausolea and Columbaria

Top two rows, left to right:
Oak Ridge Abbey, a classical mausoleum designed like a monumental public building; 1920s, Oak Ridge Cemetery, Hillside, Illinois.
Elegant, recently completed mausoleum; Trinity Cemetery, Manhattan, New York.
Huge mausoleum under construction; 1986, Queen of Heaven Cemetery, Hillside, Illinois.
A church-like mausoleum blends a warm earth color with an evocative ribbon of glass; Italian National Cemetery, Colma, California.
Harmonious interior of adjacent mausoleum: fresh flowers reveal that the space is well-visited; 1985.
Rosedale Cemetery, Linden, New Jersey.

A mausoleum can take a ten-acre cemetery and change it into a 100-acre cemetery by going up.
—Mausoleum builder, Indianapolis, 1982

6. Heavenly
5. Upper
4. Touch
3. Eye
2. Heart
1. Prayer

—Levels in mausolea run by a major cemetery conglomerate, 1987

Community mausolea, like apartment buildings, are built with several "floors"; those at the top are accessible by stairs and long corridors. On each level rows of vaults—like large drawers—are stacked six or seven high; the top row is reached by ladder. Some community mausolea contain only a few dozen crypts, while a single interconnected complex in the Queen of Heaven Cemetery in suburban Hillside, Illinois can accommodate 20,000 corpses. The project is so vast that it might be mistaken for an extension of nearby O'Hare International Airport.

For Adolph Strauch, administrator of Spring Grove Cemetery in the 1860s, "it was much more natural and appropriate to see the grass-covered graves of a family side by side, than to have them remain unmixed with the earth, deposited on stone shelves above ground and forming separate portions of preserved corruption, from which volumes of pernicious gases are continually exhaled." Strauch believed that a cemetery should increase its acreage in order to accommodate additional clientele. Yet a century later many old cemeteries have run out of space and are unable to purchase new land; for them, a community mausoleum is the only way to stay in business.

Early in the twentieth century, a New York-based corporation called The New Mausoleum offered to provide *campo santos* for many major American cities. Their elegantly bound promotional brochure declared earth burial to be repulsive, citing the "deep, dark, hole in the ground, in which the remains of the loved ones are to be hidden forever,...the certainty that the grave will be, partially at least, filled with water during every wet season,...the uncertainty that the loved ones' remains will repose in peace even there, and not...be exhumed by some ghoul, to find their way to the dissecting table,...and the awful suspicion that life may not have been extinct, and that possibly they may have been buried alive...." In contrast, their proposed palaces for the dead offered "a secure, sanitary sepulchre." Earth burial, "a crude method," was to be replaced by The New Mausoleum.

Pre-Depression era community mausolea were solidly built, with grand entrances in the lavish revival styles of the private mausolea of the wealthy, only on a much larger scale. The decor was correspondingly rich, employing colored marble, sculpted bronze doors, chandeliers, and period furniture. Tombs were situated inside the building along carpeted hallways that ended with stained-glass windows or sculpture. But today, even though their walls and floors shine clean, a chemical smell pervades the air of these imposing mausolea. Mausolea have became public buildings without a public—eerie places, light-filled, silent, and devoid of visitors or any signs of them.

Most community mausolea were built more recently, in the last three decades. Unlike earlier elite examples, they are bare and functional storage cubes whose tombs face outward. Mausolea tend to be built in stages, one building at a time, to form a complex that may include a memorial wall, a columbarium (a vault in which ashes are deposited) and space to scatter ashes. A large mausoleum complex is likely also to contain interior crypts and a chapel. Sometimes columns, overhangs, walkways, fountains, and statues are added to make these basic structures more attractive. Marble surfaces, lettering and artificial or natural flowers add a bit of color. Visitors may bring flowers to fill small attached vases, but otherwise the burial spaces are standardized. There is little visual focus with this arrangement. The rare visitors often turn away from the minimal exterior of the grave, looking lost in thought.

Facing page, bottom row, left to right:
Mausoleum blocks built like small houses, linked by pediments and walkways. The interior space has a courtyard with statues and a reflecting pool; Mountain View Cemetery, Oakland, California.

Long mausoleum in a black cemetery, with as many as eight caskets in line to fill each deep chamber; Lincoln Cemetery, Compton, California.

Memorial walls, columbaria and mausolea; Capistrano Gardens, Evergreen Cemetery, Los Angeles, California.

This page:
Mausoleum with a long skylit gallery; Mountain View Cemetery, Oakland, California. *Left*

Section of a mausoleum faced with white marble; Dade Memorial Park, Miami, Florida. *Right*

Bohemian National Cemetery

This portrait of a distinguished old man with a reflective air is enshrined in a setting of lustrous pink satin and dainty artificial flowers. *Left*

Crematorium building in the shape of a church; "The Mother Monument" by Albin Polasek in front; 1914. *Right*

And in your hands there remains but an urn of clear ashes.
—Vaclav J. Petrzelka, dedication for columbarium, Bohemian National Cemetery, Chicago, 1919

Czech-Americans, "predominantly of a rationalist ideology," were early promoters of cremation. Their columbarium, at Bohemian National Cemetery in Chicago, constitutes one of the most striking funerary spaces in America. Opened in 1919, the rooms are filled with glass-fronted, box-shaped niches containing the cremated remains of as many as eight thousand people.

Although each niche differs from the others, a shared decorum prevails. Since the Bohemian National Cemetery was organized by Czechoslovakian rationalists and freethinkers, angels, saints, views of paradise, and other Christian symbols of the afterlife are absent. Around an urn are arranged such items as photographs, artificial flowers, draped fabrics, medals, flags, poems, and even knickknacks. In addition to formal portraits, snapshots portray people at leisure in their homes and illustrate the character

of their earthly surroundings. The concentration of the variety of motifs within a small space intensifies the brief glimpses offered into the lives, beliefs and aspirations of the deceased. The niche interior has a crowded, somewhat domestic feeling, with a background of tufted white or pastel satin and a profusion of silk blossoms and small flower pots.

The placement of photographs within the niches follows important patterns. For example, the portraits of different family members are usually the same size and arranged according to the chronology of deaths. Unlike family tombstones, where the position of names and images is permanent, in niches the memorial to the most recently deceased person may be placed closest to the viewer. Photographs of those who died young are generally given prominence.

As the columbarium niches at Bohemian National Cemetery sold rapidly, an extension was constructed by 1948. But "to insure a more impressive appearance" in the new section, the administration ruled that only flowers could be used as decoration and then only in the spaces provided outside the niches. These newer columbaria exude a cold, impersonal spirit now standard in this type of burial space. Preserving the image of an American community of Czech descent, and something of their taste and feelings as well, the original niches speak of the deceased with an eloquence no longer found in today's all but anonymous columbaria.

In rows, left to right:

Niche in a patriotic mode with an American flag. A sailor killed in World War II holds the center place. Stars and the inscription "1943" are engraved on the urn.

A profusion of flowers and photographs obscure the funerary urn.

The serious face of a young woman, amidst full-length portraits of older family members, lends intensity to a display.

In the most exclusive section of the columbarium, large niches are surrounded by carved wooden frames; inside, the lavish urns double as monuments.

Accompanying the metal boxes of ashes are the faces of young and old, male and female, formal and relaxed, old country and American.

Within locked niches, cremation urns shaped as jars and boxes are decorated with popular motifs: flames, wreaths and cala lilies.

Conclusion

Overleaf:
1793, Mount Pleasant Cemetery, Newark, New Jersey. *Left*
1913, Lutheran Cemetery, Queens, New York. *Right*

I declare and pronounce—that henceforward, and for all time to come, this ground belongs not to the living, but to the dead!
—The Honorable D. D. Barnard, consecration address, The Albany Rural Cemetery, 1844

Whatever the cause, one consequence is clear: the places where we bury our dead are no longer important parts of the landscape we inhabit.
—Catherine Howett, "Living Landscapes of the Dead," *Landscape*, 1977

The contemporary isolation of the cemetery is a post-World War II phenomenon that reflects a diminishing sense of mortality as an organizing principle in the United States. In contrast to Mexico, where the extinction of life is a common theme in songs, fiestas, proverbs, and popular beliefs, the United States is a nation where youthfulness is everywhere celebrated. Contemporary cemeteries are out of touch with an American culture that is relentlessly cheerful. The heavy old entrances and monuments do not find an echo in our modern minds. The once-assertive expressions of faith in the resurrection seem naive. The place of the cemetery in everyday life is denied by neglect and erosion. Even the idea of the grave as an inviolate resting place does not attract eager defenders. With this altered value system, burial places have become necessary nuisances, not central institutions, in the life of a community. Indeed, the developers of one of the nations's oldest and most famous planned communities, Columbia, Maryland, simply forgot to include a cemetery. Not until the town had grown beyond 70,000 residents was 28 acres set aside for Columbia Memorial Gardens. And reflecting a shift of attitude throughout the nation, above-ground monuments were forbidden, replaced with bronze markers flush with the grass.

Nineteenth-century guides to large cities typically devoted several pages of text and maps to cemeteries. By 1989, guidebooks referred only to burial grounds of the rich and famous; landscapes and monuments went unmentioned. A qualitative change in our perception of the cemetery is exemplified by two accounts, separated by more than a century, of Green-Wood Cemetery. In the 1873 edition of *Wood's Illustrated Handbook to New York*, Green-Wood is described as being "at the present one of the largest and perhaps the most beautiful cemetery in the world; it commands, also, splendid views of the city and harbor." In the 1983 *Blue Guide, New York*, the cemetery is portrayed as "...a popular outing spot for Victorians who liked taking fresh air in a funeral atmosphere." While the first account of Green-Wood assumed that a general public would want to visit, the second limits the interest to a restricted public —those preoccupied with things funereal or old-fashioned and strait-laced.

In the nineteenth century one could purchase individual guides to a number of elite cemeteries. The nineteenth-century guide to Mount Auburn Cemetery, for example, went through at least twenty editions and included engravings of Cambridge City Hall and historic structures of nearby Harvard College. Similarly, *Smith's Illustrated Guide to and through Laurel Hill Cemetery* (1852) contained a section on commercial and industrial buildings, integrating the bustling central business district of Philadelphia with the quiet resting place of the dead.

In the nineteenth-century conception of the cemetery, the grave was a place to rekindle powerful memories, a place to flee for solace and counsel when that of the living fell short. Even at the dinner table, death was a common subject.

Florid writings stressed "the sanctity of the burial ground" and the importance of the cemetery for family and community. In 1873, Wilson McCandles wrote about Allegheny Cemetery: "On these grounds the ripe fruit and the faded leaf of human growth...await the mysterious change by which this corruptible body will put on incorruption and this mortal [creature] will be clothed with an immortal existence. This profound mystery meets and confronts us at the gates of the cemetery, and at the grave's mouth." The 1844 inaugural address of Albany Rural Cemetery similarly predicted a spiritual life after death: "It is indeed a rest from labor—a repose after a long and difficult journey, but it is more than this. The worn and wearied body is laid away in the earth, to undergo that great mystic change which must fit it for the resurrection. 'It is sown a natural body, it is raised a spiritual body.'"

The nineteenth-century cemetery held a place in the civic affairs of its community. When Jenny Lind, "the Swedish Nightingale," gave a concert in Bridgeport in the 1850s, for example, the receipts were used to build the stone archway of Mountain View Cemetery. And an 1873 account of Pittsburgh's Allegheny Cemetery boasted that it "[had] already risen in public estimation to the rank of a highly useful institution, and it [was] considered by all an ornament and honor to the city."

Monument dealer's display, Queens, New York. Too expensive to erect and prohibited by many cemeteries, statues such as these no longer sell; 1986.

The cemetery also functioned as a forum to publicize grievances and to right wrongs. In Chicago's Oak Woods Cemetery, for example, a large late nineteenth-century stone cenotaph bears a lengthy dedication that reads in part:

To those unknown heroic men,
Once residents in the Southern states,
Martyrs for human freedom,
Who at the breaking out of the Civil War
Refused to be traitors to the Union...
This stone is raised and inscribed,
After thirty years of waiting,
By one of themselves,
An exiled abolitionist.

For the anonymous Unionist who erected this eloquent memorial, the cemetery provided a space with which to address future generations.

Similarly, a nineteenth-century grave could announce a covenant. Alexander Milne (died 1838), through a will carved into his tombstone, left a fortune to found homes for destitute orphans (St. Louis Cemetery, New Orleans). William Lewis Morgan (died 1930) used the cemetery as a podium from which to announce his most cherished beliefs. He enjoined citizens of America to "Ever protect and hold sacred: the bible, the home, the common schools and the Republic" (Rosedale Cemetery, Los Angeles).

Immigrant cemeteries in particular offered their sponsoring communities a physical space to document the cohesiveness of their society. Bohemian National Cemetery, once at the center of Czechoslovakian community life in Chicago, typifies such cemeteries. Its monuments and buildings are named after great events in Czech history, such as the fifteenth-century martyrdom of Jan Hus and the twentieth-century election of Thomas G. Masaryk as the first president of the Czechoslovakian Republic and signer of its Declaration of Independence. Bohemian National celebrates the immigrants' integration into American society as well. Symbols of Americanism mix harmoniously with reminders of Czech pride. A large monument lists the names of soldiers of Czech descent who lost their lives in American wars. For more than half a century Bohemian National Cemetery contributed to the support of an orphanage and a home for the aged located nearby and helped to defray the cost of the weekly "Rationalist Radio Hour." The entire community once gathered in the cemetery for important political rallies. At the inauguration of the Masaryk Mausoleum in 1960, Czech songs were intermingled with Cold War speeches, and the Czechoslovakian immigrants celebrated with prominent politicians like Senator Paul Douglas and Governor Otto Kerner. The contemporary cemetery of the 1980s, by contrast, has lost the functions of cultural participant, public forum, community institution, and visible embodiment of its neighborhood's values.

The cemetery, as an American institution disconnected from the people it is intended to serve, shares its fate with the church, the family and the public school. But in these other cases, television shows, the press and conferences arouse public attention and discuss the shape of the new institutions most likely to replace the older ones. By contrast, the change in American attitudes towards death, burial and cemeteries has not been much analyzed. Only occasionally does the mass media remark upon curious aspects of cemeteries and call attention to vandalism and abandonment.

Many factors are responsible for the declining significance of the cemetery. The invention of the photograph, for example, diminished the need to visit the grave in order to remember a close relative. Similarly, a sharply declining twentieth-century death rate has not only reduced the number of childhood tragedies but also generally delayed the loss of parents until a time when their long lives can be considered complete; although these deaths require commemoration, the intensity of mourning is diminished. Also, since Americans move more frequently than they used to, the graves of parents and other ancestors often get left behind in communities from which survivors have become detached both mentally and physically. Finally, forgetfulness plays a role. As a mausoleum builder put it, "after thirty years a grave gets cold." Many older cemeteries have run out of burial space, and few people still alive remember anyone buried there. With this, the entire place ends up "cold."

The devaluation of commemoration in the context of the cemetery is not limited to sociological factors. The commemorative nature of the cemetery has been physically diminished as well, especially in regard to the number of funerary sculptures. Individually commissioned statues carry expensive price tags. According to an Italian-American monument maker in Queens, New York, the proliferation of statues in the 1920s stemmed from their affordability. At the time, an American sculptor's wages averaged between five and ten dollars a week; markers and statues could also be easily imported from Carrara. A hand-carved, life-sized figure cost about $40. (In 1989, even if a sculptor could have been found to do the same quality of work, the price would have been closer to $2,000.) Not only do many cemeteries forbid such statues, but installation of a large figural monument in a cooperative cemetery is very costly. Not surprisingly, the demand for funerary sculpture is slight. Even mass-produced, sand-blasted, granite images of religious figures are relatively unpopular. As a monument maker explained, now "people want luxuries like a bigger house or a new car, ...priests do not promote religious statues,...families are not interested in them,...cemeteries are forgotten,...people think these statues are junk."

The evocative nature of cemetery monuments is further threatened by neglect and erosion. Cemetery maintenance crews cart broken statues, uprooted monuments and fences away from the grounds. This thinning out of vertical markers erases the sense of commemoration and reduces burial grounds to the landscapes of flat memorial parks.

The meaning of markers is often lost even before serious physical deterioration takes place. Cemetery records ordinarily do not reveal when a marker was placed on the grounds, where it was made or who the sculptor was, let alone any description of the intended message.

Yet some still sense a certain power in statues. The elderly caretaker of New Lots Cemetery in Brooklyn, New York, for example, could not bear to discard the faded and broken images of the Virgin Mary and Christ that had been deposited on the grounds by neighborhood people. When asked about these statues—which are not from the graves themselves but are laid to rest in the cemetery—he first denied their presence, saying, "That is just nothing," but then added, "When they get ugly enough I will throw them out." When the wind blows them down, he picks them up, freely admitting that he hates to throw them out: "They're religious stuff."

Markers, rail fences, tombstones, planters, and fragments of statues lie discarded in a huge pile; Lutheran Cemetery, Queens, New York, 1988.

Broken and faded Roman Catholic statues, placed on the grounds of the Dutch Reformed New Lots Cemetery; Brooklyn, New York, 1988.

Most cemeteries are vast democracies of the dead. There, ordinary people—"the undistinguished dead"—for the first time can write in stone and preserve for a century or longer their names, dates, epitaphs, allegiances, and likenesses in the open air, above their mortal remains. For those who know the family, the plot is a shrine for remembrance. Many die with the small consolation that they will be buried with their loved ones, their graves visited by their descendants; family plots, visible millions of times in vast, collectively-created landscapes across the country, testify to the comfort in this understanding. An article appearing in an 1897 issue of *Park and Cemetery* noted that durable monuments and headstones "in all coming time...tell to generations yet unborn that you once lived."

More than remembrance, the cemetery derives power from the intuitive belief that the dead persist, that they have not vanished altogether from our world, that they communicate with the living, that something of their life force resides where the body is buried or, to a lesser degree, where the ashes are deposited. Once this belief weakens, the cemetery loses its significance, becoming an unsettling and unwanted reminder of mortality.

In 1896 *Park and Cemetery* recalled that the "oldest form of worship was that of deceased ancestors whose spirits were supposed to forever haunt the ancient hearthstone and tomb." This intuition of an ongoing, mystical life in the grave is central to Thornton Wilder's play, *Our Town*, of 1938. Recently, in William Kennedy's novel *Ironweed*

(1983), the dead of Albany's Saint Agnes Cemetery speak to each other and mysteriously attract the living. Francis Phelan, the story's protagonist, finds—without even searching for it—the grave of his son Gerald, dead for twenty-two years, whose burial place Francis has never visited. Instinctively, father is drawn to son.

Historian Paul Robinson, on the other hand, argued in 1981 that the contemporary "neglect of death—its reduction 'to the insignificance of an ordinary event' is a measure of our psychic maturity. We all know that, like all biological creatures, we must come to an end....I see nothing lost—and much gained—in [death's]...relegation to the periphery of human existence." That a respected historian does not consider death "a great central fact of life, whose proper management is essential to happiness" or necessary for our conception of maturity and wisdom is symptomatic of profound changes in American attitudes.

The heyday of the traditional American cemetery lasted only about a century, and as this book has shown, its era is coming to an end. Yet, in these times of ambiguity and uneasiness about the meaning of death and the afterlife, the bereaved still need spaces where they can reflect upon loss and feel comfortable nurturing the memory of the dead. The shape of such places in this age of changed resources and values is, as yet, unknown.

Concrete burial vaults, designed to prevent the earth from caving in around the coffin, lined up, ready for use; Los Angeles, California, 1987.

Bibliography

Adams, Henry. *The Education of Henry Adams*. Boston: Houghton Mifflin, 1918.

Allegheny Cemetery. *Welcome to a Tour of Allegheny Cemetery*. Pittsburgh, n.d. Brochure.

American Cemetery, The Magazine of Cemetery Management, 1980–1987.

Ames, Kenneth L. "Ideologies in Stone: Meanings in Victorian Gravestones," *Journal of Popular Culture* 14 (Spring 1981): 641–656.

Andrews, Wayne. *Architecture, Ambition and Americans*. New York: Vintage, 1947.

Aries, Philippe. *The Hour of Our Death*. Translated by Helen Weaver. New York: Knopf, 1981. Originally published as *L'Homme devant la mort*. Paris: Editions du Seuil, 1977.

———. *Images of Man and Death*. Translated by Janet Lloyd. Cambridge, MA: Harvard University Press, 1985.

Bailey, Conrad. *Harrap's Guide to Famous London Graves*. Foreword by Sir John Betjeman. London: Harrap, 1975.

Bandiera, John D. "The City of the Dead: French Eighteenth-Century Designs for Funerary Complexes," *Gazette des Beaux Arts* 101 (January 1983): 25–33.

Barber, Paul. *Vampires, Burial and Death: Folklore and Reality*. New Haven, CT: Yale University Press, 1988.

Baudier, Roger. *St. Roch Chapel and the Campo Santo of New Orleans*. New Orleans: New Orleans Archdiocesan Cemeteries, 1975.

Becherer, Richard. "Placing the Dead: Burial Sites in Early Boston, and Beyond," *Modulus* 17 (1984): 85–105.

Bellefontaine Cemetery. *A Journey Through History: Touring Bellefontaine Cemetery*. Saint Louis, 1983. Brochure.

Bender, Thomas. "The Rural Cemetery Movement: Urban Travail and the Appeal of Nature," *New England Quarterly*

47 (June 1974): 196–211.

Benes, Peter. *The Masks of Orthodoxy: Folk Gravestone Carving in Plymouth County, Massachusetts, 1689–1805*. Amherst, MA: University of Massachusetts Press, 1977.

Benrimo, Dorothy. *Camposantos*. Fort Worth, TX: Amon Carter Museum of Western Art, 1966.

Berck, Judith. "Remembrance and Poverty: The Road to Potter's Field." New York, Coalition for the Homeless, May 1986. Mimeo.

Bergman, Edward F. *Woodlawn Remembers: Cemetery of American History*. Utica, NY: North County Books, 1989.

Bigelow, Jacob. *A History of the Cemetery of Mount Auburn*. Boston: J. Munroe, 1860.

Bloch, Maurice, and Jonathan Parry, eds. *Death and Regeneration of Life*. Cambridge, Engl.: Cambridge University Press, 1982.

Bowman, Le Roy. *The American Funeral*. Washington, DC: Public Affairs Press, 1959.

"A Brief History of Calvary Cemetery." New York, Calvary Cemetery, [1979]. Typescript.

Brown, Frederick. *Père-Lachaise: Elysium as Real Estate*. New York: Viking, 1973.

"Burial," *North American Review* 93 (1861): 108–136.

The Cemetery Handbook: A Manual of Useful Information on Cemetery Development and Management. Chicago: Allied Arts Publishing, [1920–9].

Christovich, Mary Louise, ed. *New Orleans Architecture III: The Cemeteries*. Gretna, LA: Pelican, 1974.

Churchill, Henry W. *Churchill's Guide through the Albany Rural Cemetery*. Albany, NY: Henry W. Churchill, 1857.

Clark, H.F. "Eighteenth Century Elysiums," *Journal of the Warburg and Courtauld Institutes* 6 (1943): 165–189.

Cleaveland, Nehemiah. *Green-Wood Cemetery: A History of the Institution from 1836 to 1864*. New York: Anderson and Archer, 1866.

Culbertson, Judi, and Tom Randall. *Permanent Parisians: An Illustrated Guide to the Cemeteries of Paris*. Chelsea, VT: Chelsea-Green, 1986.

Curl, James Stevens. *A Celebration of Death*. New York: Scribners, 1980.

———. *The Victorian Celebration of Death*. Detroit: Partridge Press, 1972.

Daly, Laura C. "A Change of Worlds: A History of Seattle's Cemeteries," *Portage* 5 (Winter-Spring 1984).

———. "A History of Evergreen-Washelli's First Hundred Years," *Portage* 5 (Winter-Spring 1984).

Darnall, Margaretta J. "The American Cemetery as Picturesque Landscape: Bellefontaine Cemetery, St. Louis," *Winterthur Portfolio* 18 (Winter 1983): 249–269.

Darnton, Robert. "The Art of Dying," *The New York Review of Books* (May 13, 1982).

"De Mortuis," *Scribners Magazine* (June 1912).

Deetz, James. *Small Things Forgotten*. New York: Anchor Press, 1977.

Douglas, Ann. *The Feminization of American Culture*. New York: Knopf, 1977.

———. "Heaven Our Home: Consolation Literature in the Northern United States, 1830-1880." In *Death In America*, edited by David E. Stannard, pp. 45–58. Philadelphia: University of Pennsylvania Press, 1975.

Douglass, David B. *Exposition of the Plan and Objects of the Green-Wood Cemetery*. New York: Narine and Co., 1839.

Downing, Andrew Jackson. "Public Cemeteries and Public Gardens," *The Horticulturalist* 4 (July 1849): 345–351.

Draper, John W. *The Funeral Elegy and the Rise of English Romanticism*. New York: New York University Press, 1921.

Dye, Nancy Schram, and Daniel Blake Smith. "Mother Love and Infant Death, 1750–1920," *The Journal of American History* 73 (September 1986): 329–353.

Enright, D.J., ed. *The Oxford Book of Death*. Oxford: Oxford University Press, 1983.

Etlin, Richard A. *The Architecture of Death: The Transformation of the Cemetery in Eighteenth Century Paris*. Cambridge, MA: MIT Press, 1984.

———. "Landscapes of Eternity," *Oppositions* 8 (Spring 1977).

Farrell, James J. *Inventing the American Way of Death: The Development of the Modern Cemetery, 1830–1920*. Philadelphia: Temple University Press, 1980, pp. 99–145.

"Fashion in Funerals and Graveyards," *The Southern Review* (October 1877).

Forbes, Harriette. *Gravestones of Early New England and the Men Who Made Them, 1653–1800*. Boston: Houghton Mifflin, 1927.

Forest Lawn Memorial Parks. Glendale, CA, Forest Lawn Memorial Parks Association, 1968. Brochure.

Francaviglia, Richard W. "The Cemetery as an Evolving Cultural Landscape," *Annals of the Association of American Geographers* 62 (1971): 500–502.

French, Stanley. "The Cemetery as Cultural Institution: The Establishment of Mount Auburn and the Rural Cemetery Movement," *American Quarterly* 26 (March 1974): 37–59.

Garland, Robert. *The Greek Way of Death*. Ithaca, NY: Cornell University Press, 1985.

Gay, John, and Barker Felix. *Highgate Cemetery: Victorian Valhalla*. London: John Murray, 1984.

Geertz, Clifford. *The Interpretation of Culture*. New York: Basic Books, 1973.

Gillespie, Angus J. "Gravestones and Ostentation: A Study of Five Delaware County Cemeteries," *Pennsylvania Folklife* 19 (Winter 1969).

Gillon, Edmund V. *Victorian Cemetery Art*. New York: Dover, 1972.

Glittings, Clare. *Death, Burial and the Individual in Early Modern England*. London: Routledge, Chapman, and Hall, 1988.

Gondolfo, Henry A. "New Orleans Cemeteries." Paper presented to the Genealogical Research Society of New Orleans, April 8, 1965.

Gorer, Geoffrey. *Death, Grief, and Mourning in Contemporary Britain*. Garden City, NY: Doubleday, 1965.

Gray, Thomas. "Elegy Written in a Country Churchyard." 1751. In *Penguin Book of English Pastoral Verse*, edited by John Barrell and John Bull, pp. 327–331. London: Penguin Books, 1974.

Greenman, Frances. "Who is Who in the Village Cemetery," *The Ladies' Home Journal* 25 (March 1908): 14.

Grinstein, Hyman B. *The Rise of the Jewish Community in New York*. Philadelphia: 1945.

Habenstein, Robert N., and William M. Lamers. *Funeral Customs the World Over*. Madison, WI: University of Wisconsin Press, 1969.

Hammond, Ruth. "A Stroll in Lakewood Cemetery," *The Minneapolis Tribune*. Reprint. Minneapolis, Lakewood Cemetery, [1988]. Brochure.

Hannon, Jr., Thomas J. "Nineteenth Century Cemeteries in Central West Pennsylvania," *Proceedings of the Pioneer America Society* (1973): 23–38.

Heaton, Claude. "Body Snatching in New York City," *New*

York State Journal of Medicine 43 (October 1945): 1861–1865.

Hinkel, John Vincent. *Arlington: Monument to Heroes*. Englewood Cliffs, NJ: Prentice-Hall, 1970.

Historical Sketch of Graceland Cemetery. Chicago, Graceland Cemetery, n.d. Brochure.

"A History of Mount Carmel Cemetery," Hillside, IL, Mount Carmel Cemetery, [1961]. Typescript.

"How the Rich are Buried," *The Architectural Record* 10 (July 1900): 22–52.

Howett, Catherine. "Living Landscapes for the Dead," *Landscape* 21 (1977): 9–17.

Huizinga, Johan. *The Waning of the Middle Ages*. Translated by Fred Hopman. New York: Doubleday, 1954.

Hunter Warren, Nancy. "New Mexico Village Camposantos," *Markers* 4 (1987): 115–125.

Huntington, Richard, and Peter Metcalf. *Celebrations of Death: The Anthropology of Mortuary Ritual*. Cambridge, Engl.: Cambridge University Press, 1969.

Hurtig, Judith W. "Death in Childbirth: Seventeenth Century English Tombs and Their Place in Contemporary Thought," *The Art Bulletin* 65 (December 1983): 603–615.

Jack, Phil R. "A Western Pennsylvania Graveyard, 1787–1967," *Pennsylvania Folklife* 17 (Spring 1968): 41–48.

Jackson, J.B. "From Monument to Place," *Landscape* 17 (Winter 1967–68): 24–25.

———. *The Necessity for Ruins*. Amherst, MA: The University of Massachusetts Press, 1980.

Jeane, Donald G. "The Traditional Upland South Cemetery," *Landscape* 18 (Spring/Summer 1968): 39–41.

Jones, Barbara. *Design for Death*. London: Andre Deutsch, 1967.

Jordan, Terry G. *Texas Graveyard: A Cultural Legacy*. Austin, TX: University of Texas, 1982.

Kallas, Phil. "The Carvers of Portage County Wisconsin, 1850–1900," *Markers* 2 (1983).

Kennedy, William. *Ironweed*. New York: Penguin Books, 1984, pp. 1–20.

Kleinberg, S.J. "Death and the Working Class," *Journal of Popular Culture* 11 (Summer 1977): 193–209.

Koch, Robert. *Louis C. Tiffany: Rebel in Glass*. New York: Crown Publishers, 1964.

Krakora, James W. *Bohemian National Cemetery Association: The First 100 Years*. Cicero, IL: Bohemian National Cemetery, 1977.

Kubler-Ross, Elizabeth. *On Death and Dying*. New York: Macmillan, 1969.

Lanclot, Barbara. *A Walk Through Graceland Cemetery*. Chicago: Chicago School of Architecture Foundation, 1977.

Lesy, Michael. *Wisconsin Death Trip*. New York: Pantheon, 1973.

Lincoln, Levi. *An Address Delivered on the Consecration of the Worcester Rural Cemetery*. Boston: Dutton and Wentworth, 1838.

Linden-Ward, Blanche. "Death and the Garden: The Cult of Melancholy and the 'Rural' Cemetery," Ph.D. diss., Harvard University, 1981.

———. "Putting the Past under Grass: History as Death and Cemetery Commemoration," *Prospects* 10 (1986): 279–313.

———. *Silent City on a Hill: Landscapes of Memory and Boston's Mount Auburn Cemetery*. Columbus, OH: Ohio State University Press, 1989.

———. "The Willow Tree and Urn Motif: Changing Ideas About Death and Nature," *Markers* 1 (1979–1980): 149–155.

Lindenwood: Place of History, Natural Beauty. Fort Wayne, IN, Lindenwood Cemetery, [1988]. Brochure.

Lotus International 38 (1983).

Loudon, John C. *On the Laying Out, Planting and Managing of Cemeteries, and on the Improvement of Church Yards*. London: Longman, Brown, Green, and Longmans, 1843.

Loughlin, C.J. "Cemeteries of New Orleans," *The Architectural Review* 103 (1948): 47–52.

Ludwig, Alan I. *Graven Images: New England Stonecarving and its Symbols, 1650–1815*. Middletown, CT: Wesleyan University Press, 1966.

Lynn, Stuart M. *New Orleans*. New York: Bonanza Books, 1949.

McCandles, Wilson. *Allegheny Cemetery*. Pittsburgh: Bakewell and Marthens, 1873.

McGrath, Robert L. "Death Italo-American Style: Reflections on Modern Martyrdom," *Markers* 4 (1987): 107–113.

Marion, John Francis. *Famous and Curious Cemeteries*. New York: 1977.

Mitford, Jessica. *The American Way of Death*. New York: Simon and Schuster, 1963.

Morley, John. "Sepulture and Commemoration." In *Death, Heaven and the Victorians*, 52–62. Pittsburgh: University of Pittsburgh Press, 1971.

Moss, Elizabeth. "Community Cemeteries Make a Comeback," *Conserve Neighborhoods* 50 (July/August 1985).

Mount Auburn Cemetery. *Mount Auburn Cemetery Guide*. 20th ed. Boston: Moses King, 1885.

———. *The Picturesque Pocket Companion, and Visitor's*

Guide to Mount Auburn. Boston: Otis and Broaders, 1839.

Nelson, Thomas C. *It's Your Choice: The Practical Guide to Planning a Funeral*. Glenview, IL: American Association of Retired Persons, 1983.

"Ornamental Cemeteries," *Yale Literary Magazine* 21 (November 1855).

Panofsky, Erwin. *Tomb Sculptures: Four Lectures on its Changing Aspects from Ancient Egypt to Bernini*. New York: Abrams, 1964.

Parkes, Colin Murray. *Bereavement: Studies of Grief in Adult Life*. New York: International Universities Press, 1973.

Penny, Nicholas B. *Church Monuments in Romantic England*. New Haven, CT: Yale University Press, 1977.

Phelps, Henry P. *The Albany Rural Cemetery*. Albany, NY: Phelps and Kellogg, 1893.

Pike, Martha W., and Janice Gray Armstrong, eds. *A Time to Mourn: Expressions of Grief in 19th-Century America*. Stonybrook, NY: Museums at Stonybrook, 1980.

Pincus, Lily. *Death and the Family*. New York: Vintage, 1975.

Platt, Carolyn V. "Prairie Remnants of the Darby Plains," *Timeline* 1 (October 1984): 46–53.

Prestiano, Robert. "The Example of D. Aldo Pitassi: Evolutionary Thought and Practice in Contemporary Memorial Design," *Markers* 2 (1983).

Price, Larry W. "Some Results and Implications of a Cemetery Study," *The Professional Geographer* 18 (July 1966): 205.

Proctor, Richard A. "The Pyramid of Cheops," *The North American Review* 136 (1883): 257–269.

Ragon, Michel. *The Space of Death: A Study of Funerary Architecture, Decoration, and Urbanism*. Translated by Alan Sheridan. Charlottesville, VA: University Press of Virginia, 1983.

Rainey, Reuban. "The Memory of War: Reflections on Battlefield Preservation." In *The Yearbook of Landscape Architecture: Historic Preservation*, 68–9. New York: 1983.

Reed-Mullins and Associates. *Cemeteries as Open Space Reservations*. Washington, DC: U.S. Department of Housing and Urban Development, 1970.

Remes, Naomi R. "The Rural Cemetery," *Nineteenth Century* 5 (Winter 1979): 52–55.

Richardson, James B., and Ronald C. Carlisle. "The Archaeological Significance of the Mausoleums in the Allegheny and Homewood Cemeteries of Pittsburgh: A Preliminary Statement," *Markers* 1 (1979–1980).

Robinson, Paul. "Five Models for Dying," *Psychology Today* (March 1981): 85–88.

Rosenblat, P.C., R. Walsh, and A. Jackson. *Grief and Mourning in Cross Cultural Perspective*. New Haven, CT: HRAF Press, 1976.

Rotundo, Barbara. "Mount Auburn: A Proper Boston Institution," *Harvard Library Bulletin* 22 (July 1974).

———. "The Rural Cemetery Movement," *Essex Institute Historical Collections* 109 (July 1973) 231–40.

Roueche, Berton. "A Reporter at Large: Marble Stories," *The New Yorker* 62 (October 27, 1986): 100–15.

Schuyler, David. "The Evolution of the Anglo-American Rural Cemetery: Landscape Architecture as Social and Cultural History," *Journal of Garden History* 4 (July–September 1984): 291–304.

———. *The New Urban Landscape: The Redefinition of City Form in Nineteenth-Century America*. Baltimore, MD: Johns Hopkins, 1986.

Sears, Roebuck Catalogue. 1905.

Seymour, William Wood. *The Cross in Tradition, History and Art*. New York: G.P. Putnam and Sons, 1898.

Sharf, Frederic A. "The Garden Cemetery and American Sculpture: Mount Auburn," *The Art Quarterly* (1961): 80–88.

Simon, Donald. "Green-Wood Cemetery and the American Park Movement." In *Essays on the History of New York City: A Memorial to Sydney Pomerantz*, edited by Irving Yellowitz, 61–77. Port Washington, NY: Kennikat Press, 1978.

Sloan, David. "The Living Among the Dead: Reflections of a Changing American Culture." Ph.D. diss., Syracuse University, 1984.

Slusarenko, Ronald. "Necrotecture: The Underground Population Explosion and its Impact on Cemetery Design," *Landscape Architecture Quarterly* 60 (July 1970): 293–300.

Smith, R.A. *Smith's Illustrated Guide to Laurel Hill Cemetery*. Philadelphia: Willis P. Hazard, 1852.

Stannard, David E. "Calm Dwellings," *American Heritage* 30 (August–September 1979): 42–55.

———. "Death and the Puritan Child," *American Quarterly* 26 (December 1974): 456–76.

———. *The Puritan Way of Death: A Study in Religion, Culture, and Social Change*. New York: Oxford University Press, 1977.

Stannard, David E., ed. *Death in America*. Philadelphia: University of Pennsylvania Press, 1975.

Stilgoe, John R. *Common Landscape of America, 1580-1845*. New Haven, CT: Yale University Press, 1982.

Street, A.L.H. *American Cemetery Law*. Madison, WI: Park and Cemetery, 1920.

Thomas, Jack W., and Ronald A. Dixon. "Cemetery Ecology," *Natural History* 82 (March 1973): 60–67.

Victor, Ralph G. "An Indictment for Grave Robbing at the Time of the 'Doctors' Riot,' 1788," *Annals of Medical History* 3 (1940): 366–70.

A Visitor's Guide to the Beauty and History of Spring Grove. Cincinnati, OH, Spring Grove Cemetery, n.d. Brochure.

Vovelle, Michael. *Ville des Morts: Essai sur l'imaginaire urbain contemporaine d'après les cimetieres Provençeaux.* Paris: Presses Universitaires de France, 1983.

Waite, Frederick C. "Grave Robbing in New England," *Medical Library Association Bulletin* 33 (1945): 272–94.

Walsh, Edward R. "Cemeteries: Recreation's New Space Frontier," *Parks and Recreation* 10 (June 1975): 28–29, 53–54.

Ward, William J., and Margaret C. Ward. "The Green-Wood Cemetery" *The Journal of Long Island History* 12 (Fall 1975).

Warner, W. Lloyd. "The City of the Dead." In *The Living and the Dead: A Study of the Symbolic Life of Americans*, 280-320. New Haven, CT: Yale University Press, 1959.

Watson, James L., and Evelyn S. Rawski, eds. *Death Ritual in Late Imperial and Modern China*. Berkeley: University of California Press, 1988.

Waugh, Evelyn. "Death in Hollywood," *Life Magazine* 23 (September–October 1947): 73–74, 83–87.

———, *The Loved One*. Boston: Little, Brown and Co., 1948.

Weisser, Michael R. *A Brotherhood of Memory*. New York: Basic Books, 1985.

Whitman, Walt. *The Portable Walt Whitman*. Edited by Mark van Doren. Revised by Malcolm Cowley. New York: Penguin Books, 1977.

Wilson, Samuel, Jr., and Leonard W. Huber. *The St. Louis Cemeteries of New Orleans*. New Orleans, St. Louis Cathedral, 1963. Brochure.

Wolfe, Kevin. "Visible City," *Metropolis* (September 1985): 44–50.

Zanger, Jules. "Mount Auburn Cemetery: The Silent Suburb," *Landscape Magazine* 24 (1980): 23–28.